Assessing the need for Access Arrangements during Examinations

A Practical Guide

Sixth Edition

Written & Edited by

Lia Castiglione

ASSESSING THE NEED FOR ACCESS ARRANGEMENTS DURING EXAMINATIONS – 6th EDITION

Copyright © Patoss 2021

ISBN: 978-0-9539315-6-9
First published 2021

British Library Cataloguing in Publication Data
A catalogue entry for this title is available from the British Library.

The book can be purchased from our website: www.patoss-dyslexia.org

Additional copies of this book may be ordered from
Patoss Ltd
PO Box 10
Evesham
Worcestershire
WR11 1ZW

Telephone: 01386 257808

Email: info@patoss-dyslexia.org

Published by

Patoss

The Professional Association of Teachers of Students
with Specific Learning Difficulties Ltd
P O Box 10, Evesham, Worcestershire, WR11 1ZW
Tel:
01386 257808

Email: info@patoss-dyslexia.org
Website: www.patoss-dyslexia.org

In furthering good practice, we are very pleased to publish this sixth edition of 'A Practical Guide'. It has been written to support the Joint Council's regulations and provide a 'how to' guide in approaching the entire area of exam access arrangements for students with specific learning difficulties (SpLD) in schools and colleges. Published in association with the Joint Council for Qualifications, this book builds on the success of the earlier editions. It is an essential resource for anyone involved in the process and replaces all previous editions.

Patoss, The Professional Association of Teachers of Students with Specific Learning Difficulties, was formed in 1987 and is now an international association of teachers and other professionals working in the field of specific learning difficulties with individuals across the educational spectrum from primary to adult. Our mission is to help people with Specific Learning Difficulties (SpLD) succeed in their education and workplace by nurturing the professionals who teach, assess and support them.

Membership is open to teachers with approved qualifications in SpLD, students working towards an SpLD qualification, other professionally qualified individuals, and all schools, colleges or organisations with a professional interest in SpLD and those who have an interest in SpLD and wish to support the aims and activities of Patoss.
Among the services we provide are:

- an e-mail helpline to assist with queries relating to SpLD assessment and practice
- a mentoring service providing personalised support in all aspects of assessment
- professional indemnity insurance scheme for appropriately qualified members
- facilities for DBS checks
- SpLD Assessment Practising Certificates and Teaching Practising Certificates
- Tutor / Assessor Index
- a range of other publications including a resources guide, bulletins and newsletters
- a website with useful information for the public and members
- SpLD continuing professional development events

We are delighted to once again work with the JCQ in bringing you this valuable updated resource and look forward to continuing to do so in the future.

Lynn Greenwold, OBE
Chief Executive

Joint Council for Qualifications

The Joint Council for Qualifications (JCQ) was formed in January 2004 and replaced the JCGQ. The JCQ consists of AQA, City and Guilds, CCEA, NCFE, OCR, Pearson, SQA, and WJEC, the largest providers of qualifications in the UK, offering GCSE, GCE, Entry Level, Functional Skills and Vocational qualifications.

The JCQ was formed to enable the member awarding bodies to act together to provide, wherever possible, common administrative arrangements for schools, colleges and other providers. In this respect the small team at the JCQ act as a hub for the joint and collaborative work of the members.

All joint regulations, guidance, forms, other administrative documents and online systems are produced through collaborative working and are introduced and used with the agreement of the members. The JCQ works with the awarding bodies to develop and agree the regulations and arrangements. The JCQ badge is used to denote where the awarding bodies have acted together.

The JCQ and the awarding bodies have worked together for many years to produce and update the regulations and guidance for access arrangements. Each year the regulations and guidance are reviewed and developed in light of best practice.

In recent years the JCQ regulations have been updated to take account of the Equality Act 2010 and the introduction of Access Arrangements Online (AAO).

The JCQ is pleased to continue to work in association with Patoss to produce further guidance for SENCos and assessors. This Guide provides invaluable information and will help to ensure that candidates are appropriately supported and receive the access arrangements to which they are entitled, thereby maintaining fairness across the examinations system.

Nick Lait
Head of JCQ Examination Services

Table of Contents

Acknowledgements

I am greatly indebted to the author of the first three editions of this Patoss Guide, **Gill Backhouse**, and to the author of the fourth edition, **Anwen Jones**.

Thank you to all those who have contributed to the 6th edition of this Patoss Guide, both in providing material and ideas and in helping to ensure that the information contained in this guide is a clear and helpful accompaniment to the JCQ regulations and guidance.

Contributors to the sixth edition

Lia Castiglione has been teaching and supporting learners of all ages for over 25 years and in varying educational settings. She is a director of SASC, the SpLD Assessment Standards Committee, and is Head of Training at Communicate-ed. Lia is a leading trainer on access arrangements and consults with the JCQ and test publishers on matters relating to specific learning difficulties and assessment. She is the co-creator of the Patoss AAA: Assessing for Access Arrangements course. Lia is highly experienced in all aspects of access arrangements, has held a current Assessment Practising Certificate since 2008 and regularly assesses in schools and colleges.

Nick Lait has provided a preamble to the 6th Edition in Chapter 1 and has contributed throughout this Guide to the interpretation of the regulations. Nick is the Head of Examination Services at the JCQ, where his responsibilities include the annual production of the JCQ access arrangements regulations, oversight of the Access Arrangements Online system and support to schools and colleges through training events and advice and guidance in regard to access arrangements. He is also the Chair of the JCQ Special Requirements Committee.

Louise Green has contributed to the chapter on gathering centre-based evidence and completing Form 8 Part 1 (Chapter 6). Louise has worked as a Specialist Teacher and Assessor since 1989, when she first joined Patoss and was a National Patoss Board Member for many years. She had been involved with access arrangements since 1990 and has assessed thousands of students over the years from a variety of schools. She has also worked as a trainer for Patoss covering several topics including access arrangements.

Caroline Read and **Gurinder Grewal** have contributed a chapter on access arrangements for students who have English as an additional language (Chapter 18).
Caroline is a Specialist Teacher who has practical experience in all areas of the Access Arrangements process and trains for LAs, Universities and SEN Services. Her work has been published by the TES and the RNIB, and she has worked with a number of publishers to develop tests. Caroline has been involved with various Ofqual and DfE training/policy projects.

Gurinder holds a master's degree in SpLD which included in-depth research into the identification of effective assessment procedures for EAL students. She has spent 20 years specialising in the tuition and assessment of students with SpLD and has supported EAL students of all levels as well as mentoring and training new teachers.

Lynn Greenwold is Patoss Chief Executive, and current Chair of SASC, the SpLD Assessment Standards Committee. She has provided valuable encouragement in bringing this new edition to fruition.

Introduction

"Much has changed" was the opening sentiment of previous editions of this Guide, but few would have predicted the changes that have been encountered, and the challenges that have been presented, in the last two academic years.

The Covid-19 pandemic has impacted on all aspects of life, including education, and this has resulted in a number of changes to practice:

- In periods of total 'lockdown', schools were closed to most learners.
- Learners working at home have not had easy access to teaching assistants or LSAs who would usually provide support for reading and writing in the classroom.
- Technology, including lessons via video link, has been used more widely.
- Learning bubbles and ongoing Covid-19 testing have caused further disruption to normal routines, including periods of self-isolation and home learning for entire groups when a learner within a bubble has tested positive for the virus.
- Social distancing, mask wearing and new hygiene regimes have added additional challenges.
- External exams were cancelled and Teacher Assessment Grades (TAGs) have been used to award grades in GCSE and GCE exams.

The impact of the Covid-19 pandemic on individual learners and to the education system itself is likely to continue to be felt for some time.

However, the principles guiding access arrangements remain unchanged. They seek to support candidates to show their knowledge and skills whilst maintaining the integrity of the qualifications they subsequently gain. These access arrangements are a fundamental part of the support for learners with learning difficulties, including SpLDs, but they only a part. Learning support and study skills support to develop independent skills must still be the primary goal. Providing such support can be a challenge, especially in periods of change and when there is immense pressure on resources, but I hope this Guide supports continued best practice and helps to promote an equitable system for all.

As with previous editions, the convention of referring to all teachers and assessors as though they were female and all candidates as though they were male has been followed. In line with the KCQ AARA document, the term SENCo has been used to refer to the person within the centre who takes the lead on the access arrangements process.

Forms and templates introduced in this book are downloadable from the Patoss website. A list of these resources and how to access them is described in Appendix 2.

Thank you to everyone who has contributed to this publication.

Lia Castiglione
July 2021

Part 1

Foundations in Access Arrangements

1. The JCQ Regulations and Guidance - Essential Reading

Each autumn the Joint Council for Qualifications (JCQ) publishes a revised document setting out its regulations and guidance for the forthcoming academic year: *Access Arrangements and Reasonable Adjustments (AARA)*. The document relates to examinations leading to qualifications from JCQ members. The AARA document, along with the other JCQ publications, such as the *Instructions for Conducting Examinations (ICE)*, is available as an interactive document through the Centre Admin Portal (CAP), which is accessed through the awarding bodies' secure extranet sites. It can also be downloaded in pdf format from the JCQ website (www.jcq.org.uk). Changes to the previous edition are highlighted in yellow.

All personnel involved with candidates who have access arrangement needs must have access to their own copy of the **current** regulations. The Patoss Guide supports, but does not replace, the JCQ AARA publication which is the primary reference and must be carefully read and followed. This edition of the Guide has been written in accordance with the regulations for 1st September 2021 – 31st August 2022. Updates to accompany the book, which will be available from the Patoss and JCQ websites, will be provided in subsequent academic years to reflect any further changes at that time. No responsibility is taken by Patoss, the editor, or the contributing authors for any misunderstandings or failure to comply with the JCQ regulations during this, or subsequent years.

The Patoss Guide is no substitute for reading the full JCQ AARA document each year.

Access arrangements are available to candidates with disabilities and learning difficulties. Whilst this guide covers the requirements for each of these groups, it focusses primarily on assessing and meeting the needs of learners with cognition and learning needs. This process often requires an assessment conducted by an appropriately qualified access arrangements assessor. The assessor's role is to work with the centre and to contribute to the required data by providing evidence of learning difficulties, not to make a decision on access arrangements themselves; an important point for independent practitioners approached directly by candidates or their parents.

Applications for candidates sitting many Level 2 and 3 qualifications are managed through the Access Arrangements Online (AAO) system. Centres must maintain a file of evidence for each candidate with approved access arrangements. A number of arrangements do not require formal evidence but they will still reflect the candidate's normal way of working and be appropriate to their needs. Access arrangements in Functional Skills examinations are dealt with directly by the relevant awarding body.

Regardless of changes to administration or adjustments to regulations, the over-arching principle to support equality of access to assessment remains the same. Discussions of the principles, systems and evidence requirements involved in achieving this goal are to be found in this Guide.

Preamble *by Nick Lait*

Previous editions of this Patoss Guide have been greatly appreciated by both assessors and the JCQ, who have found it an invaluable resource in giving advice to those assessing candidates for access arrangements. Those working within the JCQ or an Awarding Body (AB) are laymen and women in this field, yet are often the first port of call for SENCos and assessors faced with difficulties.

Patoss and the JCQ have been working with each other for many years with the aim of strengthening the working relationship between centres and the JCQ/Awarding Bodies so access arrangements can effectively meet the needs of candidates while maintaining the integrity and validity of qualifications. It is the JCQ's key aim that the qualifications of a candidate with access arrangements should be seen to have the same credibility as those of any other candidate. In order to do that, we have to make sure that all candidates meet the same requirements in examinations and are assessed in exactly the same way.

The move towards greater inclusion has seen more and more access arrangements being processed by centres. The Disability Discrimination Act (DDA) and the Equality Act (2010), which superseded the DDA, both made arrangements more equitable across all types of disability.

In September 2008 the process of applying for access arrangements was revamped, being modernised for the 21st century. Access Arrangements Online (AAO) was introduced allowing applications to be processed online, with a single instant decision. This online system has significantly reduced paperwork and bureaucracy for centres. 90% of applications are approved automatically by the system, with the evidence kept on file within the centre for inspection purposes. Since September 2009, the JCQ has removed 17 access arrangements from AAO, allowing SENCos to simply make the decision as to whether the candidate needs the arrangement(s).

To inform all decisions SENCos and assessors **must** read the JCQ regulations carefully each year. So often people rely on or misinterpret what someone else has told them and then find themselves in difficulties when 'an inspector calls'! Please do not leave yourself without adequate evidence that the candidate **is** eligible for the arrangement, especially those processed online which you have subsequently allowed.

We hope that you will use this book alongside the JCQ regulations as well as AAO. They complement one another and need to be used together. As the JCQ regulations change slightly every year you **must** keep constantly up to date with changes in order to give the best service to your candidates.

2. Understanding & Implementing the JCQ Regulations

Finding your way

One of the problems when beginning any discussion about access arrangements is that we are entering a world of jargon, which can lead to confusion and, sometimes, misunderstanding. Often people think that they understand the various roles and issues until they try to have a conversation, or until a scenario crops up that they haven't encountered previously. We will consider the personnel involved and the terminology that can be associated with access arrangements.

Roles and responsibilities - an overview

The Whole-Centre Approach

In days gone by, staff within schools and colleges tended to view access arrangements as a 'special needs' issue to be dealt with by the SENCo or the learning support department, and nothing at all to do with subject teachers.

Whilst this may have been an accepted viewpoint historically, the access arrangements process can no longer work in this way. The JCQ regulations emphasise that there must be a 'whole centre approach' to access arrangements and reasonable adjustments. The *Introduction* of the JCQ AARA document calls for such an approach and states that senior centre staff, including the head teacher, members of the senior leadership team and the SEN Governor (where relevant), as well as the SENCo and assessor, must be familiar with the entire contents of the JCQ AARA document.

A range of people will be involved in the access arrangements process, each person with their particular role to play. There needs to be effective communication between the various parties involved in the process in order for it to run smoothly and successfully.

The Candidate

This is the person taking the examination, in other words, the 'learner' or 'student.' The term 'candidate' applies to all genders, young and old and is the term used in the JCQ AARA publication and by centres when entering learners for external examinations. It is, therefore, the preferred term used in this context.

The candidate should be encouraged to inform teaching staff as soon as possible during the course if he is having difficulties with learning or in need of support. He may, for example, be having difficulties with completing work within the expected time, taking far longer than peers to complete homework, using friends to help with reading and spelling tasks, or borrowing friends' books to catch up with work that was not able to be completed in lessons.

When a candidate moves to a new setting, such as moving from an 11-16 school to a further education college, he should ensure that he discusses any previous support and access arrangements he received with the relevant staff member in the new setting.

The Parent/Carer

This is the person with personal responsibility for the candidate.

Parents and carers can have a role to play in the access arrangements process. If they have concerns over their child's learning, they should arrange to discuss these with the SENCo or equivalent member of staff in FE for follow-up in school or college. This may be even more relevant in recent times because periods of home-schooling may have alerted parents to their child's learning needs and they may have acted in a supporting role, for example, by providing support for reading or spelling. If an external assessment is considered, the parents should also discuss this with the centre, so that the correct procedures for access arrangements assessments can be maintained.

Much valuable time is wasted if parents try to by-pass the regulations and engage in a personal battle with the JCQ or an Awarding Body, or commission an external report for access arrangements without prior consultation with the centre. The JCQ and the Awarding Bodies will not deal directly with parents.

The way to achieve the best possible outcome for the candidate is to make sure everyone knows how to proceed and the processes that must be maintained. The centre having a clear and well-publicised policy on access arrangements will help to ensure that parents understand the evidence requirements for access arrangements and that the correct procedures are followed.

The SENCo (or an equivalent member of staff within a FE college)

The term SENCo is used throughout the JCQ publications and refers to the person within a centre who has responsibility for special educational needs and/or learning support. Within school and college settings, this role is given a variety of titles, including SENCo, SENDCO, ALNCO, Learning Support Coordinator, Head of Additional Support, and other similar terms. The JCQ recognises that, particularly in a further education college, the term SENCo is not generally used and so the AARA document also refers to an 'equivalent member of staff in a FE college'. Throughout this Guide, the term SENCo has been used to reflect the wording of the JCQ AARA.

The SENCo takes the lead on access arrangements within a centre and will coordinate the entire process. The SENCo's duties will be discussed throughout this Guide. They include:

- Identifying learners who may need access arrangements;
- Collating information from a range of sources, including feedback from teaching and support staff;
- Completing JCQ Form 8 Part 1 or the Centre File Note for candidates requiring access arrangements that need approval;
- Arranging for candidates to be assessed and providing the assessor with the centre-based evidence through JCQ Form 8 Part 1;
- Storing access arrangements information on candidates within the centre;
- Presenting information to the JCQ Centre Inspector, upon request;
- Determining the access arrangements for a candidate, ensuring that the agreed arrangements meet the published criteria;
- Processing applications online or, where the Examinations Officer processes applications, being available to oversee the process;
- Working with teaching staff and exams office staff to ensure that access arrangements are put in place for internal school tests, mock exams and external examinations.

The Access Arrangements Assessor

The JCQ requires that assessments for access arrangements are carried out by suitably qualified professionals. The Head of Centre (see below) is responsible for appointing assessors, and the JCQ sets out the criteria that must be adhered to in order for an assessor to be deemed suitably qualified (See Chapter 7).

Ideally, the SENCo will also be the in-house Access Arrangements Assessor, provided that she is appropriately qualified. However, it is perfectly acceptable for the SENCo and the Access Arrangements Assessor to be different people. In this case, they will need to work together to ensure that the process is joined-up and consistent.

The Access Arrangements Assessor's role will be discussed in detail in Chapter 7. Briefly, the assessor will:

- Provide the centre with evidence of their qualifications before assessing the candidate;
- Obtain JCQ Form 8 Part 1 from the SENCo prior to assessing the candidate;
- Assess the candidate in those areas necessary to gain appropriate evidence for access arrangements, taking account of the information within Part 1;
- Report the results of the assessment in JCQ Form 8 Part 2;

- Sign and date the final page of Part 2 to confirm that the assessment has been conducted by the Access Arrangements Assessor personally.

In addition to conducting assessments, an Access Arrangements Assessor working directly within the centre is able to complete JCQ Form 8 Part 1 and to process access arrangements applications online.

The Head of Centre

The Head of Centre is the head teacher or principal within a school or college and carries ultimate responsibility for the quality of the access arrangements process within the centre. This is why it is essential for the Head of Centre to be familiar with the access arrangements process and the contents of the JCQ AARA document.

The Head of Centre is responsible for appointing the Access Arrangements Assessor following the criteria within the AARA document. The appointment process includes obtaining evidence of the assessor's qualification either through a copy of a qualification certificate or from a print out of the assessor's listing on the HCPC, SASC, Patoss or Include-ed website.

Another responsibility of the Head of Centre is to ensure that those who are employed to facilitate access arrangements, including adults acting as readers and scribes, are appropriately trained and fully understand the rules of a particular access arrangement. This task is often delegated to the Examinations Officer, but it is the Head who carries ultimate responsibility.

The Senior Leadership Team (SLT)

The JCQ AARA document states that members of the Senior Leadership Team must be familiar with access arrangements procedures and the contents of the JCQ AARA publication. Members of the SLT can help in the gathering of evidence from teaching staff. This can be especially helpful if a subject teacher is reluctant or slow to provide feedback. If the SENCo is not available when the JCQ Centre Inspector calls, a member of the SLT can present the access arrangements evidence in place of the SENCo. There must, therefore, be liaison between the SENCo and the SLT member to ensure that the evidence that is held on file is understood and can be presented to the JCQ Centre Inspector effectively.

Teaching Staff and Support Staff

The Subject Teacher is the person who teaches the candidate a particular subject. The teacher may need to provide the Examinations Officer with the details of the examinations that are to be entered in each series. The Subject Teacher may need to seek or give advice about the reasonableness of the adjustment or arrangement in the context of an assessment objectives being tested in the qualification.

Support staff have titles such as a Teaching Assistant (TA), Higher Level Teaching Assistant (HLTA), Learning Support Assistant (LSA), Learning Mentor and Support Teacher. Support staff can run support sessions for learners to attend within a learning support department or can work in the classroom to support particular students in accessing the curriculum by providing help with tasks such as reading, spelling and writing. Some support staff are linked directly with one learner through dedicated funding, whilst others provide more general support for learners with needs.

Teaching and support staff are often the people who know the candidate best, in terms of their learning needs, within the centre. They will need to provide the SENCo with relevant information to inform JCQ Form 8 Part 1 or the Centre File Note.

Teaching staff should ensure that learners with access arrangements have appropriate support within class lessons, tests and internal exams so that access arrangements reflect the candidate's normal way of working. Whilst some arrangements, such as a word processor or a coloured overlay, can be used in lessons and examinations in the same way, this does not necessarily mean that the candidate will have exactly the same support arrangements in the classroom and in examinations.

It would not always be possible, for example, for a candidate requiring 25% extra time in examinations to have longer in lessons to complete work, although extra time could be provided for class tests and to respond to oral questions and work could be modified or fewer questions set. In addition, there will be adjustments made to take account of the candidate's difficulty, such as handouts being provided instead of having to copy from the board. Similarly, it would not be realistic in most settings for a candidate using a reader or a scribe in examinations to have these arrangements in all lessons. However, appropriate support or adjustments for reading and writing will be in place in the classroom.

Any concerns about a learner should be referred by teaching and support staff to the SENCo. These may include, for example, a student needing help with reading or writing; slow or illegible handwriting; behavioural issues such as poor concentration; consistently taking longer than expected with set tasks and running out of time in tests and exams. Such concerns should be brought to the SENCo's attention in good time so that there is sufficient time to investigate them and, where appropriate, collate centre-based and assessment evidence and make an application for access arrangements before the published deadline. Early identification will also mean that the access arrangements can be established as the learner's normal way of working.

If a learner does not make use of a suggested access arrangement in a particular subject, teaching staff should also feed this back to the SENCo for further investigation.

The Examinations Officer

It could be said that the SENCo prepares for learners to have access arrangements in exams, whilst the Exams Officer is responsible for facilitating the exams, including making the entries and administrating the use of access arrangements.

The JCQ Instructions for Conducting Examinations (ICE) booklet sets out the information that is required by the Exams Officer including, for example, the conditions that must be complied with for maintaining the security of the examination papers.

The Exams Officer will work with the SENCo to ensure that access arrangements are in place for internal examinations, including mock exams, and to ensure that all access arrangements are applied for online before the published deadlines so that permission is in place before an access arrangement is given in external exams.

In addition, the Exams Officer needs to arrange to have the required number of trained Invigilators and examinations support staff (for example, readers, scribes). The Exams Officer works with the SENCo to ensure these personnel fully understand their roles and the rules that govern their behaviour.

Another important duty of the Exams Officer is to arrange to have sufficient resources such as word processors and examination reading pens available. For students who require examinations on coloured, enlarged or single-sided paper, the Exams Officer ensures that the papers are prepared by printing out from a pre-ordered PDF into the format required or by photocopying. Any cover sheets that are needed, for example for candidates using scribes, are provided to the invigilator by the Exams Officer prior to the exam commencing.

The Invigilator and other Examinations Staff

The Invigilator is responsible for conducting an examination session appropriately so that all candidates have an equal opportunity to demonstrate their abilities. It is the Invigilator's responsibility to ensure the security of the examination and prevent possible candidate malpractice or administration failures.

Some access arrangements require a responsible adult to facilitate the arrangement during an examination. These can include a reader, scribe, practical assistant, prompter, language modifier and communication professional for candidates using sign language. In examinations where a candidate and a scribe, a reader or a practical assistant are accommodated in a separate room on a one-to-one basis, the invigilator may also act as the scribe, the reader or the practical assistant.

The use of a language modifier (LM) is considered by the JCQ to be a high-risk access arrangement. The Invigilator has a specific role to play when an LM is used. There must be a separate Invigilator for each LM and the Invigilator must listen carefully and observe the conduct of the LM throughout the exam. The Invigilator is required to countersign the LM cover sheet ensuring that it accurately reflects the actions of the LM during the exam.

The Awarding Body (AB)

This used to be called an Examinations Board. It is the organisation responsible for producing the examination papers, grading the candidates' work and issuing the results. Some access arrangements require approval direct from the Awarding Body, including 'high risk' access arrangements that are referred to the relevant Awarding Bodies via Access Arrangements Online and Functional Skills examinations that require a paper application for access arrangements.

The AB has a duty, under the Equality Act 2010, to make reasonable adjustments when the assessment arrangements (i.e. examinations) would put a disabled candidate at a substantial disadvantage compared with a non-disabled candidate. Access arrangements are the main way in which the AB makes reasonable adjustments.

The Joint Council for Qualifications (JCQ)

The ABs work together through the JCQ, which has its own director and staff. The JCQ publishes a common set of rules to make sure access arrangements are appropriate and consistent. The JCQ AARA document contains these rules.

JCQ Centre Inspectors visit examination centres to check the evidence for access arrangements that have been approved for candidates within the centre.

The Regulators

Each country in the UK has a qualifications regulator who is responsible for ensuring that ABs carry out their work according to agreed procedures, such as General Conditions of Recognition and Qualification Level Conditions and Requirements. The regulators for general qualifications are OFQUAL (England); Qualifications Wales (Wales) and CCEA (Northern Ireland).

Remember, the candidate who gets the best deal is the one in a setting that takes a whole-centre approach, where parties understand their particular role in the process and work together as a team, in an organised and timely manner, coordinated by the SENCo.

What does the terminology mean?

Access Arrangements	These are arrangements, or adjustments, that are made before the examination, such as 25% extra time or allowing the candidate to use a scribe. They are based on need and must reflect the candidate's normal way of working in the centre. They must also meet the requirements of the assessment. The candidate gains marks for skills he can carry out, so the arrangement must not allow anyone else to do something which will gain marks for the candidate.
Access Arrangements Online (AAO)	The online system for processing access arrangements that require JCQ or Awarding Body approval.
AARA	The JCQ regulations and guidance document, *'Adjustments for candidates with disabilities and learning difficulties, Access Arrangements and Reasonable Adjustments.'* The AARA publication is updated annually and can be accessed via the Centre Admin Portal (CAP). In addition, the AARA can be downloaded from the JCQ website: www.jcq.org.uk
Access Arrangements Assessment	This is the testing that is carried out by a suitably qualified assessor to gather assessment evidence for a particular access arrangement that a candidate requires. For example, the assessor may carry out a test of spelling accuracy for a candidate who requires a scribe in examinations.
Access Arrangements Assessment Report	JCQ Form 8 Part 2 is used to report the results from an access arrangements assessment. This is sometimes known as the access arrangements assessment report. [Note: this is **not** the same as a diagnostic assessment report.]
Appeals	If the centre is not satisfied with the grade(s) or the special consideration awarded, the Examinations Officer may ask the Awarding Body for further explanation. The Head of Centre may then wish to take the matter to the Appeals Committee of the Awarding Body involved. The Appeals Committee is made up of independent people who are not employed by the Awarding Body. They cannot change the regulations, but they can ensure that the decision has been made according to the rules and the agreed procedures and is fair and consistent. Only the Head of Centre can make an appeal.

Assessment	This word includes written examinations and non-examination assessment, which are two different types of assessment. It also includes practical tests and speaking tests.
Assessment Objectives	These are the knowledge, understanding and skills being tested in the assessment. They might include how much geography the candidate knows but also how well the candidate can analyse a set of geographical data. They might also include how well the candidate can speak French or model clay or build a working machine.
Awarding Body	The organisation responsible for setting and awarding qualifications that are taken in secondary schools and colleges. (See above.)
Candidate	The learner taking examinations. (See above.)
Centre	The school or college where the examination is to take place, i.e. the registered examination centre. This is normally the place where the course has been taught.
Entries	These are technically the orders for the question papers and other materials. The Examinations Officer submits them by fixed deadlines. It is very important to meet the deadlines if the question papers are to arrive in time. For specifications that include them, entries will also include non-examination assessments (NEAs) so that marks can be submitted.
Examination Series	These are the months when examinations are timetabled and, where applicable, non-examination assessment marks have to be submitted.
In-house assessor	An access arrangements assessor who is employed by the centre to carry out assessments and complete JCQ Form 8 Part 2. The in-house assessor may also be the SENCo. The assessment will usually take place within the centre but may be conducted at a different location (or remotely).
Independent assessor (also known as an external assessor)	An assessor who is commissioned by a learner, a learner's parents or another agency that is not the centre to carry out an assessment. An independent assessor must be accepted as an assessor by the centre **before** the assessment takes place if the results are to be used for access arrangements.

Malpractice	If the JCQ or an Awarding Body is not satisfied that the assessment has been carried out according to the regulations and believes that access arrangements have given the candidate an unfair advantage, the Head of Centre may be asked to carry out an investigation. The outcome can vary from a warning to the removal of a centre's registration.
Reasonable Adjustments	Reasonable adjustments are measures that are put in place to remove barriers that disabled people face. They are required by law for candidates who are disabled under the terms of the Equality Act 2010 and who would be at a disadvantage compared with non-disabled candidates. Access arrangements are the main way in which Awarding Bodies make 'reasonable adjustments' in line with the Equality Act 2010.
Referral	If AAO rejects an application for an access arrangement, the case can be referred online to the Awarding Body. A careful review of the regulations is essential before a referral is made.
Regulations	Every year the JCQ publishes a booklet of regulations and guidance relating to access arrangements. This document is known as the AARA (see above).
Responsible adult	This is the adult who acts in a supporting role to a candidate in examinations. The responsible adult may act as a reader, a scribe, a communication professional, a practical assistant, a prompter or a language modifier. In each case, there are strict rules that must be adhered to. In some cases, the same responsible adult may act in more than one of these supporting roles (or as an invigilator) during an examination as long as permission has been granted for each arrangement.
Results	The results are based on the marking of each part of the assessment. All candidates have to be measured according to the same mark scheme so that their results have the same value. Those with access arrangements receive valid results as long as all the regulations have been followed.
Special Consideration	This is a small adjustment to the marks given when the candidate knows the work but is too ill at the time of the assessment to show what he or she can do. It cannot compensate for not being able to carry out the tasks being tested or missing large sections of the course. The procedures for special consideration are detailed within a separate JCQ document.

What are the deadlines that must be met?

Access arrangements will ideally be put in place as early as possible for a candidate so that he has plenty of opportunity to practice using the arrangements and they become his normal way of working throughout the course. For the arrangements that require approval, the JCQ publishes deadlines by which applications must be made for candidates taking exams in the next examination series. These are found in the AARA document.

The JCQ also issues deadlines for the ordering of modified papers, such as Braille papers. Because these papers are prepared individually it is essential to make the application by the published deadline to guarantee the candidate has the required papers for his examinations.

Why do the Regulations change?

There are several reasons why the regulations have changed over the years. Some are simply for practical reasons, some have their roots in changes of thinking resulting from research undertaken by the regulators, some have arisen through changes in disability legislation and others as a consequence of AAO and centre inspections.

Over the years, centres have sought clarification about how to interpret the regulations, so amendments are made to help to clarify or simplify some of the sections which have prompted enquiries.

The JCQ consults with representatives from disability groups in an attempt to understand the challenges faced by disabled candidates and efforts have been made to accommodate the needs of the various groups of learners as far as possible without changing the integrity of the assessments and the qualifications those candidates will obtain.

Equality Act 2010

The Equality Act 2010[1] is a single legal framework that streamlines disability legislation to protect people from discrimination. Disability is a 'protected characteristic' under the Act. A person is considered to have a disability if they have a physical or mental impairment that has a substantial and long-term negative effect on that person's ability to carry out normal day to day activities. In simple terms, 'substantial' means that the effect is more than minor or trivial and 'long-term' means lasting 12 months or more.

---

[1] Department for Education (2014) The Equality Act 2010 and Schools Departmental advice for school leaders, school staff, governing bodies and local authorities. Available at:
https://www.gov.uk/government/publications/equality-act-2010-advice-for-schools [Accessed: 3 July 2021].

Awarding bodies have a duty under the Equality Act 2010 not to discriminate against individuals with protected characteristics when conferring qualifications, with regard to developing specifications, identifying the assessment criteria and drafting question papers. The duty for an awarding body to make a reasonable adjustment will apply where assessment arrangements would put a disabled candidate at a substantial disadvantage in comparison with a candidate who is not disabled. In such circumstances, the awarding body is required to take reasonable steps to avoid that disadvantage. Access arrangements are the main way in which an awarding body complies with the Equality Act 2010 duty to make 'reasonable adjustments.'

The Equality Act 2010 applies in England and Wales. Separate disability legislation is in place in Northern Ireland although the definitions and procedures set out in the JCQ AARA document that relate to access arrangements and reasonable adjustments will still apply.

SEND Code of Practice: 0 - 25 years

The SEND Code of Practice: 0 to 25 years[2] applies in England. It is statutory guidance for organisations working with and supporting children and young people with special educational needs (SEN) and disabilities.

Within the SEND Code of Practice, children and young people are defined as having special educational needs if they have a learning difficulty or disability that requires special educational provision to be made for them. Many learners with SEN require access arrangements. Disabled children and young people may not have SEN but are covered by the SEND Code of Practice as well as by the Equality Act 2010.

The SEND Code of Practice instructs that where a child or young person is covered by SEN and disability legislation, reasonable adjustments and access arrangements should be considered as part of their SEN planning and review.

---

[2] Department for Education and Department of Health (2015) Special educational needs and disability code of practice: 0 to 25 years. Available at: https://www.gov.uk/government/publications/send-code-of-practice-0-to-25 [Accessed: 3 July 2021].

3. Principles Underlying Access Arrangements

The underlying rationale for access arrangements is very clear. They exist to provide reasonable adjustments to allow equality of access to assessment in education. They aim simply to allow candidates the opportunity to **'show what they know and can do without changing the demands of the assessment.'**[3] They must not confer an unfair advantage to those who receive them, and credit cannot be given for skills that cannot be demonstrated. All involved in the process should ensure that the principles of access arrangements are upheld in order that the integrity and credibility of qualifications and arrangements are maintained.

Given this principle, access arrangements can be awarded to those with a special educational need (SEN), a disability or a learning difficulty. The potential effects of such disabilities and difficulties during examinations, as well as everyday study, vary in nature and degree. It is the responsibility of the centre to monitor students' difficulties and make appropriate arrangements in examinations.

When applying for access arrangements there are two main issues to be considered in relation to each candidate:

1. Has the candidate been entered for examinations which are at the right level, *given his level of general ability and attainment in each particular subject?*

2. What are the implications and degree of the candidate's *current difficulties* during examinations with *reading the questions* and *responding in writing* under *timed conditions*? How does he normally cope with demonstrating his knowledge and understanding? Access arrangements should reflect his usual method of working (i.e. slowly; with a reader or scribe; using a word processor; with regular breaks; etc.)

With regard to the first point, it is important that centres recruit with integrity when enrolling students onto courses. The centre should seek to ensure that a learner has the potential to complete a course of study successfully and achieve the qualifications he undertakes.

Examinations are designed to test the knowledge and skills a candidate has developed in a chosen subject area. His marks and grades show the degree to which his work has met the published assessment objectives. This will depend on a variety of factors: how well he has been taught, how much effective work he has put in over the course and his examination technique; as well as his general underlying ability and his aptitude for each particular subject. There are wide variations in accuracy and speed of reading and writing skills across

---

[3] JCQ (2021) Access Arrangements and Reasonable Adjustments, *Definitions*, available at www.jcq.org.uk

the population – as well as every other human characteristic – and such normal variance is not cause for access arrangements.

The clear message from the JCQ is that the only difficulties meriting significant adjustments to the normal examination conditions are those whose effects can be described as *substantial*, that is **not** *minor or trivial,* ***and*** long-term. In other words, a difficulty has to be demonstrated which really affects a candidate during examinations. This may be obvious, for example, when a student has extremely poor literacy skills or has major problems with concentration. However, it is important to recognise that the difficulty may be less obvious, but the effects are nevertheless more than minor or trivial, such as when a student has a persisting lack of fluency with some aspects of literacy and language (e.g. word-finding).

Substantial Difficulties

When a candidate has been identified as having substantial or severe difficulties, so long as they have been entered for an appropriate level of examination according to the knowledge and skills they have attained in that subject, it is right and proper to provide them with the help needed to show what they know and can do.

The JCQ regulations define the level at which reading and writing speed and processing difficulties are considered to be substantial, as evidenced by assessment data. Since all examinations under the jurisdiction of the JCQ are available nationally to any candidate whatever his age, cognitive ability or background, the same standards regarding 'difficulty in access' must clearly be applied to all candidates. In the case of the most common access arrangements requiring assessment evidence (25% extra time, scribe), this has been set as one standard deviation below the mean (i.e. a standard score below 85) for a candidate's age on current, nationally standardised tests. For access arrangements that are considered 'high risk,' the threshold is two standard deviations below the mean (i.e. a standard score below 70).

Centres are sometimes concerned about applying for assistance for candidates with poor literacy skills or processing weaknesses who would not necessarily be diagnosed as having a specific learning difficulty, such as dyslexia. It should be noted that a formal diagnosis of a learning difficulty that provides a 'label' is not required in all but the rarest of cases.

In addition to those with cognition and learning needs, candidates who have problems coping under standard examination conditions due to communication and interaction needs, sensory and physical needs, and social, emotional and mental health needs can also have adjustments made, appropriate to their needs, so long as there is the required documentation to confirm their difficulties.

Is the difficulty long-term?

The JCQ regulations state that both a history of need and a history of provision are required to support an application for access arrangements. Learning difficulties are generally the result of a developmental condition and, in many cases, there will be a clear and consistent history of difficulty and delay in the acquisition and development of age-appropriate basic skills. In such cases, support is likely to have been in place from early in the student's schooling and there will be no problem establishing the long-term nature of both the difficulty and the provision.

It is recognised, however, that there are candidates whose learning difficulties may not become very noticeable until curricular demands exceed their capacity to cope comfortably with their studies. In some cases – and this is often found in older students in sixth form or further education – their learning difficulties may not have been recognised as such when they were younger.

Furthermore, there may be no history of learning support in school for a variety of reasons ranging from shortage of resources to a reluctance on the part of the student to accept such help. Extra tuition may have been provided privately in some cases.

In the case of a late manifestation of a student's learning difficulty, the history of need and history of provision must still be documented by the SENCo, albeit the evidence may relate to a more compressed time period than for a student who has well-established evidence of difficulties and provision.

The thorny issue of extra time

More than any other access arrangement, the provision of extra time is the subject of much – sometimes heated – debate including, on occasion, in the national press. Part of the problem is that candidates who require extra time in examinations sometimes have literacy skills that are within the normal range. SENCos can struggle with the issue of whether extra time can be justified for a candidate with a specific learning difficulty when his literacy skills, in terms of their accuracy, are every bit as good as those of many other students.

The key to solving this problem is to consider speed (e.g. fluency and efficiency) of working to see if, and to what degree, the student is affected when working under closely timed conditions, such as in an examination, by specific processing difficulties or a difficulty in either reading or writing speed. (See Chapter 9 for the assessment criteria for extra time).

Let us consider some common scenarios:

- A candidate with a long history of specific learning difficulties has, through appropriate intervention and hard work, attained age-appropriate literacy skills within the average range and is what is sometimes referred to as a 'well-compensated' dyslexic. Although he makes spelling mistakes, these are generally minor, so his writing is quite readable, and the style and quality of content reflects his knowledge. However, he often has to re-read text several times to access the meaning and has to consider his spellings to achieve this degree of accuracy. After liaising with the candidate's subject teachers and collating the centre-based evidence, the SENCo completes Form 8 Part 1, after which an assessment takes place. The results reveal persisting and significant processing difficulties, evidenced by several below average scores. Specialist study skills support and 25% extra time during examinations are put in place for the student.

- A Year 10 student experienced some minor difficulties with spelling and reading when younger but had little or no help at primary school as he was not 'below average' and coped quite well. However, he is now becoming anxious about his impending exams. He is monitored in lessons and tests and most subject teachers report that he works slowly, particularly when longer written answers are required, and that he can be slow to get started on assignments. The student attends small-group study skills sessions to help with revision and examination technique. In the end of year tests, he is given 25% extra time. A change in pen colour for the extra time shows that he used the extra time well and gained extra marks within the extra time allowance.

  This information is documented in detail within Form 8 Part 1 and the student undergoes an access arrangements assessment with the SENCo, who is a qualified assessor. At assessment, his reading speed is found to be well within the average range but his writing speed is low average and one cognitive processing test result is also within the low average range. An application for 25% extra time is made. This is rejected by AAO and is referred to the ABs who, after examining the detailed evidence put forward, grant the use of 25% extra time in examinations.

- A student with no history of difficulties or provision in school is not living up to the expectations of his parents, or possibly his school. They believe he may do better if he has extra time. The student's parents arrange for him to be assessed without prior consultation with the school.

  The assessment results show a large difference between his general underlying ability, which is above average, and his spelling accuracy, although this is age-appropriate and well within the average range. He makes minor errors which do not impair readability. His writing speed is average, and his reading is good in all respects.

A discrepancy is also found between his underlying ability and the results of one cognitive processing subtest but none of the scores fall outside the average range and most are above the mean. He is diagnosed as 'mildly dyslexic' and the report recommends extra time.

However, the correct procedures were not followed, and the assessment evidence does not meet the JCQ assessment criteria for extra time. No extra time can be awarded to the student on the basis of the assessment results.

Many SENCos will, unfortunately, recognise the situation described in the third example. 'Readers Letters' and opinion-piece articles in the national press generally attribute it to a desire to gain an unfair advantage by those who can afford to pay for a private assessment. Indeed, abuse of the system is perceived as widespread in some quarters, so let us deal with this issue head-on.

There is a public perception that having more time to think and write confers an advantage, which may well be true for students who do not have a substantial learning difficulty or disability. Indeed, a study, in which the views of 66 'non-disabled' mock GCSE candidates in Year 11 were canvassed (Woods 2000[4]), found that:

- 71% reported running out of time in at least one examination
- 86% believed that they could have gained at least one or two more marks if they had been allowed extra time[2]

However, despite the perception that extra time confers an advantage, a recent study of 714 undergraduate students (Duncan 2021[5]), found that the average exam writing speed of students with SpLDs who had 25% extra time remained lower than that of 'typically developed' (TD) students. In fact, the writing speed of the students with SpLDs continued to be slower even when they used a word processor alongside 25% extra time. Furthermore, a comparison of the mean marks achieved showed that the SpLD group scored lower in examinations than the TD learners, despite their coursework marks being comparable.

> Giving extra time to candidates who do not have evidence of need for it and for whom such arrangements have not formed part of normal provision during school-based tests and exams constitutes malpractice. Centre staff should be mindful of the fact that they are acting for and on behalf of the ABs with regard to implementation of the JCQ regulations. Both candidate and centre may pay the cost of failing to adhere to the regulations.

---

[4] Wood, K. (2000) *'Assessment Needs in GCSE Examinations: some student perspectives' in GCSE Examinations: some student perspectives'* in Educational Psychology in Practice, Vol.16, No.2 pp131-140
[5] Duncan, K. (2021) *'Equity or Advantage? The effect of receiving access arrangements in university exams on students with specific learning difficulties'* Available at:
https://sasc.org.uk/SASCDocuments/Equity%20or%20Advantage-H%20Duncan.pdf [Accessed: 4 July 2021].

Part of the problem is that there is also a public perception that anyone with a diagnosis of dyslexia is entitled to 25% extra time in public examinations and that the professional who carries out the assessment is the one who makes the decision. This is most emphatically **not** the case. The decision to either grant or apply for access arrangements will always be made by the centre, guided by both the centre staff's own knowledge of the candidate's needs and normal way of working and the assessment paperwork produced by a suitably qualified assessor.

The joined-up approach that the JCQ calls for has strengthened the requirement for the centre to drive the access arrangements process. It is the SENCo who must arrange for a candidate to be assessed and the assessor, in-house or external, must obtain the information on the candidate's needs and normal way of working before any testing takes place.

> The question is not 'Does the candidate have dyslexia,' but 'What are the effects of his difficulties during exams, with reading the questions and responding in writing, and are there any access arrangements that will minimise these?'

It is important to note that the centre inspectors and awarding body staff do not see it as in any way appropriate to dispute diagnoses made by professionally qualified practitioners, rather to argue that '**evidence of need and normal way of working**' is the key issue.

Is the student who writes fluently but makes minor mistakes going to make fewer errors if he has more time? Can he proof-read effectively and so correct mistakes during his extra time allowance? (Since it is axiomatic that those with dyslexia cannot see where they have made mistakes, this may be unlikely!) These are questions that might be considered when gathering centre-evidence and during a careful assessment.

In contrast, if the student is slowed down when writing because he cannot think how to express his ideas in writing despite his good subject knowledge, has to re-read questions several times more than other students before he can fully understand them, and has to read back his own work repeatedly to ensure it makes sense and addresses the question, then extra time will clearly be an appropriate adjustment. Again, both feedback from subject teachers and careful assessment which includes observation of strategies is crucial.

In short, although sound evidence of a difficulty with learning is required before any access arrangements are considered, this in itself is not enough. The real issue is always 'evidence of need.'

Communication

A sustained awareness campaign may be required to fully inform candidates and their parents of the JCQ regulations and the rationale underpinning them. Teacher-led discussion and debate amongst students about special needs, disability, fairness and such issues have been found to lead to a more open and manageable attitude in some cases. Research providing statistical data about the exam performance of candidates using access arrangements can also help in advancing understanding.

It is recommended that centres issue clear and timely information to parents on the systems and procedures for access arrangements and encourage open communication so that all parties can work together and expectations are managed.

To support this aspect of the centre's responsibility, see page 86 for an example of the information to include in an introductory information sheet for parents and candidates.

In summary...

Access arrangements during examinations are available to give those candidates with difficulties which significantly affect their performance during examinations fair opportunities to demonstrate what they know and can do in each subject. No allowances can be made for shortcomings in subject specific knowledge and skills. Certificates should convey reliable information to employers, further and higher education institutions, and so on, about the candidate's attainments in each subject. Close adherence to these principles will give confidence to all in the access arrangements process.

4. Access Arrangements Available

Access arrangements need to be considered on an individual basis, subject-by-subject. As subjects and their methods of assessment vary, leading to different demands of the candidate, he may not require the same access arrangement in each specification or examination. For example, a candidate may require the use of a word processor in the examinations that require extended writing, whereas this may not be a helpful arrangement for maths papers.

Some candidates will need more than one access arrangement to help to minimise the impact of their particular difficulties, for example, the use of both a reader and a scribe, or a word processor and 25% extra time, whilst others may require an access arrangement in certain examinations but not in others.

The most commonly used access arrangements are listed within the JCQ AARA document. Some of the arrangements can be provided by the centre without having to seek permission using Access Arrangements Online. These are known as centre-delegated access arrangements. Other arrangements require permission and must be applied for and approved before they can be used in formal examinations. All access arrangements must reflect a candidate's normal way of working in the centre.

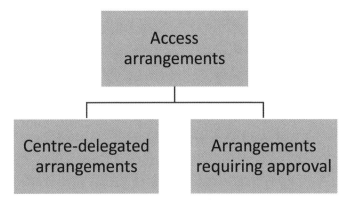

Centre-delegated access arrangements

A variety of access arrangements can be provided for candidates without permission. These arrangements do not need to be processed online and, for most of them, no formal evidence needs to be held on file. Centre-delegated access arrangements must reflect the candidate's normal way of working in the centre and can be put in place for a candidate on the basis of need.

A full list of the centre-delegated access arrangements can be found in the JCQ AARA document. The following access arrangements are centre-delegated:

Supervised rest breaks

This is a helpful arrangement for a candidate with a condition or issue that makes it difficult to complete an exam without a break, or rest period.

For some candidates, having time out of the exam is more effective in meeting their needs than a longer exam time and so supervised rest breaks need to be considered before applying for 25% extra time.

When the supervised rest break is put into effect, the timing of the exam is paused and then restarted when the candidate is ready to continue with the exam. During the rest break, the candidate must not have access to the question paper or the answer booklet. The candidate can remain seated at the desk, stand or walk around in the room, or leave the room accompanied by an invigilator.

There is no maximum set time for rest breaks and they can be awarding according to candidates' specific needs. Before the start of the exam, the SENCo will need to carefully consider the candidate's circumstances and plan with him how the rest breaks will be applied in an exam. For example, if the candidate has a condition that makes sustained concentration difficult, a decision may be made to have a break for a set amount of time, such as ten minutes in each hour. For some candidates, a blanket pre-arrangement is not appropriate and rest breaks will only become necessary if a condition flares up on the day of the exam; a plan can be agreed should this situation occur. For example, a candidate who is known to have migraines may need a plan in place to have a rest break to take medication and recuperate if an episode occurs before or during an exam.

An application does not need to be made for supervised rest breaks. However, the SENCo needs to be satisfied that the candidate has long-term, persistent and significant difficulties and that there is a genuine need for the rest breaks. The candidate's difficulties must be established within the centre and, in a school setting, will be known to his form tutor, Head of Year, the SENCo and the pastoral leader.

For GCSE and GCE candidates, the SENCo must produce written evidence in the form of a 'short concise file note' written on centre-headed paper and signed and dated. The file note confirms the candidate's established difficulties and that supervised rest breaks reflect the candidate's normal way of working in the centre. The written evidence needs to be kept in the candidate's file in readiness for the JCQ Centre Inspection. For example, for a candidate with a medical condition, such as epilepsy, the SENCo would write a file note to set out the nature of the candidate's difficulties and how they affect the candidate in examinations, detailing why supervised rest breaks are necessary. The file note would also confirm that the candidate usually has rest breaks in examinations on account of his medical condition. There may also be medical evidence to confirm epilepsy and this would be placed in the candidate's file to accompany the file note.

Separate invigilation within the centre

This arrangement enables a candidate who has an established difficulty to sit the examination in a separate room, either singly or in a smaller group. Each room in which the examination is being taken will require a separate invigilator.

This arrangement can be a suitable option for a variety of reasons, including for candidates who cannot cope with sitting exams in the main hall and need to be in a separate exam room due to severe behaviour, concentration or anxiety issues. (A candidate having 'exam nerves' would not be an appropriate justification for a separate room, as feeling nervous is a usual state of affairs when taking important examinations.) In addition, some candidates will need to be accommodated separately due to another access arrangement they are using, such as the facility to read aloud, the use of a language modifier or a communication professional for a candidate using sign language.

An application does not need to be made and no formal evidence needs to be kept on file for this arrangement.

Read aloud

Some candidates need to have the option to read aloud. Reading the question paper aloud can help the candidate to understand and process the written information it contains. In addition, a candidate having the opportunity to read back his own written responses can help with editing and proofreading his work, to check it is grammatically accurate and that the written responses answer the questions in sufficient detail.

This arrangement can be helpful for a candidate who has difficulty with reading or processing written information but who does not need a more substantial access arrangement such as a reader or computer reader or extra time.

A candidate who has approval for a reader but who cannot have this arrangement in an exam testing reading can also have the option to read aloud with a maximum of 50% extra time (the extra time being provided in place of the reader).

The facility to read aloud does not need to be applied for and no formal evidence needs to be kept on file for this arrangement.

Examination reading pen

This is a portable device that is used to scan text and hear it read aloud. The 'pen' simply reads aloud what has been scanned, it does not have a dictionary or thesaurus or any inbuilt storage facility. The use of the device promotes independent working as the candidate is in control of the exam reading pen, meaning that particular words or pieces of text can be scanned and listened to as many times as he requires. The exam reading pen can be used with earphones so that the candidate can be accommodated in the main examination hall.

As with the previous arrangement, it can be a useful option for those candidates who have reading difficulties that require some support during exams but who do not need a reader or computer reader.

An application does not need to be made and no formal evidence needs to be kept on file for this arrangement.

Prompter

The use of a prompter is an access arrangement that can be put in place for candidates who have persistent issues with concentration or distractibility. It can be a helpful arrangement for candidates who have little sense of time, who are very easily distracted, or who have problems moving on from one question to another.

The prompter is a responsible adult who uses prearranged prompts or signals to help keep the candidate focused or to move him on to the next question.

The pre-agreed signals may include saying the candidate's name or a phrase, such as the amount of time left; showing the candidate a card with a prompt phrase written on it, such as 'move on to the next question'; or tapping the desk to help to refocus the candidate. Where a candidate is accommodated separately, on a one-to-one basis, the invigilator may also act as the prompter.

An application does not need to be made and no formal evidence needs to be kept on file for this arrangement.

Coloured overlay

A coloured overlay is a sheet of transparent coloured acetate or plastic that is placed over a page of text to help make reading more comfortable. Some candidates use spectacles with coloured lenses as an alternative, or in addition, to a coloured overlay. A virtual overlay can be used by a candidate who is reading from a computer screen.

The use of a coloured overlay does not need to be applied for and no formal evidence needs to be kept on file for this arrangement.

Coloured/enlarged paper

Some candidates with visual difficulties may require adaptations to the question paper itself. There are various options that are permitted, to reflect a candidate's normal way of working.

The simplest way to prepare a question paper is for a PDF version of the question paper to be obtained. This can be printed from directly in the required format. Alternatively, the exams officer is permitted to open the question paper packet under secure conditions, within 90 minutes of the examination start time, to make copies.

The centre is permitted to make one or more of the following adjustments:

- Copy and enlarge the paper from A4 to A3
- Copy a question paper onto coloured paper
- Produce a question paper with single-sided print

Some candidates may require more than one of these adjustments to be made, such as single-sided, blue paper enlarged to A3. Any combination of these three adjustments is permitted.

An application does not need to be made and no formal evidence needs to be kept on file for this arrangement. However, it is important to note that a centre is not permitted to make any other adjustments to the examination paper. If other modifications are required these must be applied for by the published deadline through the Modified Papers area of Access Arrangements Online.

Word Processor

The use of a word processor is a centre-delegated access arrangement as long as the spell-check and grammar-check facilities and predictive text are switched off. This, effectively, makes the word processor a 'typewriter' with the candidate working independently on his spelling, grammar and punctuation.

It is important that a candidate who will use a word processor with the spell-check and grammar-check switched off in exams has ample opportunity to work with a word processor in this way. It is very different to working with a computer when these facilities are enabled, as tends to be the norm. We can come to rely on the auto-correction of misspelt words and the underlining of spelling and grammatical mistakes. When these functions are switched off, the candidate is responsible for ensuring that what has been written makes sense and is spelt correctly, with no 'typos.' This needs to be practised and to become the candidate's normal way of working. It would not be appropriate for a candidate to use a word processor in this way in examinations unless he has had extensive practice.

This arrangement can be useful for a candidate who has handwriting that is difficult to read or is largely illegible or for a candidate with slow handwriting. It can also be helpful for a candidate who has problems with planning and organising when writing by hand as it facilitates editing, meaning that the quality of written language can improve significantly.

In some centres, the curriculum is delivered through the use of IT with all learners in a year group using laptops that have been provided by the centre. Because this is the normal way of working for the candidates, the centre may allow the use of a word processor (with spell-check and grammar-check switched off) in examinations for this group of candidates.

It may be appropriate for a candidate to use a word processor in some exams, such as those requiring extended written answers, and to write by hand in other exams. This can be determined on an individual basis, according to the particular needs of each candidate.

Although individual evidence for each candidate is not required for the use of a word processor, the centre must have a policy on the use of word processors in exams that can be shared with learners, parents and carers. This policy should make it clear that the use of a word processor must reflect the candidate's normal way of working within the centre. A member of the centre's senior leadership team must also produce a written statement setting out the criteria that the centre uses for the allocation of word processors in exams. During a centre inspection, the JCQ Inspector will ask to see the statement and will want to know how this information is conveyed to learners and their parents.

Some candidates may need to use a word processor with the spelling and grammar check functions enabled. It is important to note that using a word processor in this way requires appropriate evidence to be gathered and held on file and an application to be made to gain permission for its use. This is an option that can be used when permission for the use of a scribe is obtained. See pages 46 and 47 for further information on scribe options.

The use of word processors in examinations will require careful advance planning with the centre's IT department to ensure that systems are in place for uploading question papers and source documents (where computer readers are used) and answer booklets, backup systems for candidates' work and the need for secure printing.

Further centre-delegated access arrangements include:

- Amplification equipment
- Bilingual dictionary (see Chapter 18)
- Braille transcript
- Braillers
- CCTV
- Colour naming by the invigilator for candidates who are colour blind
- Communication professional (for candidates using sign language)
- Live speaker for pre-recorded exam components
- Low vision aid/magnifier
- OCR scanner

If an access arrangement is not listed within the JCQ AARA document as a centre-delegated access arrangement (an arrangement that does not need to be applied for online), it must have prior approval and the relevant evidence held on file before it can be used in an examination.

Access arrangements requiring approval

If a candidate requires an adjustment or type of support in examinations that is not listed as a centre-delegated access arrangement, approval must be granted by the JCQ or the awarding bodies before the arrangement can be used in external examinations. See Chapter 9 for details of the assessment evidence required for each of the access arrangements. Chapter 14 deals with applying for access arrangements using the online system.

The following access arrangements must be applied for using Access Arrangements Online:

25% extra time

This is the most common access arrangement that requires approval. It can be considered for candidates who have a disability or learning difficulty that substantially impacts on their ability to work under closely timed conditions. The difficulty could be due to problems with writing speed, reading speed or the processing of information.

Candidates who have extra time in examinations can be accommodated in one area of the main exam hall, grouped together so that the minimum amount of disruption is caused to them when the other candidates leave the room at the end of the normal examination time. Sometimes a separate room is used for all the candidates within a centre who require extra time.

Before an application for 25% extra time is made, the SENCo needs to consider whether it is the best arrangement to meet the candidate's needs and whether supervised rest breaks is a more appropriate arrangement. Some candidates with severe needs may require both 25% extra time and supervised rest breaks.

It is important that a candidate who has extra time in external examinations has sufficient opportunity to practice using the extra time in tests, internal exams and mock examinations, and that the arrangement reflects his normal way of working. The candidate may need to be supported to develop strategies that make the best use of the extra time, as this may not be obvious to him.

In the classroom, whilst lessons cannot be extended by 25%, extra time can be offered, for example, to complete work and tests. Additional time can be provided to answer oral questions if needed. Other accommodations would be in place to provide support for the underlying cause of the slow speed of working. For example, the learner may be permitted to photograph the board, be provided with handouts, or be given work to copy up later instead of being required to copy down large pieces of text from the board. Many schools and colleges provide outline notes to students, which can be added to during lesson time and for homework, rather than expecting learners to make extensive notes during lecture-type lessons. Some learners may require modifications to assignments to take account of their slow working speed.

Depending on the nature of the difficulties, it may be appropriate for a candidate to have extra time in all examinations, or in some but not in others. It may not be appropriate or necessary, for example, in practical exams or in non-examination assessments. Extra time is not permitted in examinations testing the time in which a skill is performed or where timing is an explicit part of the assessment objectives, such as expressive arts, musical performances and sports.

Extra time of up to 50% (between 26% and 50% extra time)

In the vast majority of cases, 25% extra time will be sufficient for a candidate who has cognition and learning needs requiring extra time in examinations. More than 25%, up to a maximum of 50% extra time, can only be considered for such a learner if there is substantial evidence that extra time is needed and that 25% extra time has proved not to be sufficient.

For a candidate with very substantial difficulties and for whom the required evidence is in place, more than 25% (up to 50%) extra time may be required.

The SENCo will need to determine the amount of extra time that is required (e.g. 40%) and to be applied for. This will be based on evidence that is gathered in the centre. For example, in tests and internal examinations, the candidate could be asked to change pen colour at the end of the standard exam time and at set intervals to determine how the extra time is used.

Extra time over 50%

Extra time over 50% is only available in very exceptional circumstances for candidates who have a very substantial sensory or multisensory impairment. Strong justification and detailed information will be needed which details why 50% extra time is not sufficient.

Reader / Computer Reader

Some candidates with reading difficulties will have problems accessing the examination paper and reading back their own written responses. A **reader** is a responsible adult who provides support for reading during an examination. It is vitally important that the person who is acting as the reader understands the requirements of the role and is able to abide by the regulations. The JCQ AARA publication includes a suggested memory aid for a reader and annual training should be arranged by either the SENCo or the Examinations Officer.

A **computer reader** is reading software, or text-to-speech software, that is used by a candidate who has reading difficulties to read an electronic version of the question paper that has been uploaded to a computer. It will also read back a candidate's work if it has been word-processed. A computer reader does not add emphasis to text or interpret the paper. Some candidates prefer using a computer reader as it allows them to work independently and they find it easier to have a word or phrase re-read several times by a computer than having to ask a reader to do this.

To obtain an electronic question paper, the centre has two choices. Ideally, a non-interactive PDF version of the question paper is ordered by the centre and this is uploaded to the computers of all candidates requiring a computer reader. The other option is for the question paper packet to be opened up to 90 minutes before the start of the examination so that the paper can be scanned into PDF format. This must happen under secure conditions, in accordance with the JCQ rules, as any infringement could constitute malpractice.

The computer reader and reader arrangements have the same evidence requirements and they are, effectively, merged. When an application is made, reader and computer reader is a single option on Access Arrangements Online and permission extends to either arrangement or both. This means that a candidate may use a reader (or a computer reader) in all exams in which he requires reading support, or he may use a reader in some exams and a computer reader in others. If a computer reader is being used and it is unable to recognise and read an individual word, a reader is able to read the word to the candidate.

Rules for a reader

The reader, at the candidate's request, is able to:
- Read the instructions of the question paper;
- Read the questions and any other text on the question paper;
- Read back the candidate's written responses (without any emphasis on errors);
- Read numbers printed in figures as words whilst pointing to the number on the question paper, for example, 56 would be read 'fifty-six' (unless the question is asking for a number to be written in words, for example, 'write the number 56 in words);
- Decode symbols and unit abbreviations in maths and science exams for candidates who require this arrangement and where it is their normal way of working;
- Enable a vision impaired candidate to identify diagrams, graphs and tables but the reader must not give any factual information other than what is on the paper.

A reader must not:
- Advise the candidate regarding which questions to do, when to move on, nor the order in which to answer questions;

- Give any spellings other than for any words that appear on the paper;
- Explain or clarify any instructions or information on the paper;
- Repeat the instructions or questions on a paper unless the candidate requests this;
- Decode any symbols in a music exam;
- In a paper testing reading, read individual questions or text and is only permitted to read the instructions or rubric of a paper, or read back the candidate's written responses.

Reading support in examinations testing reading

To expand on the final point above, a reader is not permitted to read the questions or text in papers or sections of papers testing reading, such as the reading section of a GCSE English language paper or a modern foreign language reading paper. There are three options for providing reading support in an examination testing reading:

- For a candidate who has approval for a reader/computer reader, up to 50% extra time can be used in place of using the reader.

  If it is helpful, the candidate may read aloud whilst using the extra time allowance in place of a reader.

  Where reading and writing are being assessed in the same paper, the maximum allowance of 50% extra time is only allocated to the reading section. The total time allocated to reading (based on the number of marks allocated to the reading questions) needs to be calculated and up to a maximum of 50% is added to that time. It may be necessary to seek advice from the relevant awarding body as to how to apply the extra time allowance.

  Extra time cannot be used in place of a reader in other types of examinations or under any other circumstances.

- A computer reader can be used in papers or sections of papers testing reading, for candidates who have approval for a reader/computer reader.

- An examination reading pen can be used in papers or sections of papers testing reading. No prior approval is needed for an exam reading pen to be used.

If either a computer reader or an examination reading pen is used in an examination testing reading, the extra time of up to 50% cannot also be used in place of a reader.

25% extra time for the use of a reader

Some candidates may have difficulties that give rise to the need for 25% extra time as well as the use of a reader or computer reader. Previously, it was possible to add an optional 25%

extra time to an application for a reader or computer reader (for example, because the candidate needed to have text read to him several times) but this is no longer the case. If the candidate requires 25% extra time, this must be applied for separately with relevant evidence held on file for the reader or computer reader and for the 25% extra time.

Accommodating the use of a reader

Candidates who use a reader or computer reader in examinations are usually accommodated in a separate or smaller room so that they are not overheard and do not distract other candidates.

A reader can either work on a one-to-one basis with a candidate or one reader can be shared by a group of 3 or 4 candidates who need only the odd word or phrase to be read. If the reader is shared between a group, candidates would put up their hand when help is needed with reading. It is not acceptable for the reader to read the paper to a group at the same time.

A reader who is working on a one-to-one basis with a candidate who is accommodated separately can also act as the invigilator. Where a reader is shared between a group, a separate invigilator is needed.

Scribe / Speech recognition technology

Candidates who have difficulties with writing may require a scribe option. Approval for a scribe enables the centre to provide support for writing in a number of ways, as follows:

- **Scribe**

  A scribe is a responsible adult who writes a candidate's dictated answers. The scribe can either write by hand or use a word processor to type the dictated responses. It is vitally important that the person who is acting as the scribe understands the requirements of the role and is able to abide by the regulations. The JCQ AARA publication includes a suggested memory aid for a scribe and annual training should be arranged by either the SENCo or the Examinations Officer.

- **Word processor with the spelling and grammar check enabled**

  The use of a word processor without spelling and grammar check (effectively, a typewriter) is a centre-delegated access arrangement (see page 40). For the candidate to use a word processor with either the spell-check or grammar-check or both switched on, there must be an approved application for a scribe.

- **Word processor with predictive text, spelling and grammar check enabled**

  An approved application for a scribe enables the candidate to use a word processor with the spelling and grammar-check switched on, and with predictive text enabled.

- **Speech recognition technology with predictive text**
  The candidate uses the computer software to dictate into a word processor (speech-to-text software). A screen reader (text-to-speech software) can also be used to read back and correct the candidate's dictated answers.

- **Computer software producing speech which is used to dictate to a scribe.**
  This is technology used by a candidate who has a physical difficulty meaning that he is not able to write or speak.

For all of the scribe options above a scribe cover sheet must be completed and submitted.

Word processor – two different access arrangements:

Centre-delegated	Scribe alternative
Word processor with grammar and spelling check switched off (effectively a typewriter) Word processor cover sheet needed for some ABs	Word processor with grammar and spelling check enabled (with or without predictive text) Scribe cover sheet used

Modern foreign language (MFL) papers
The use of a scribe is not permitted in MFL papers unless the candidate dictates the foreign words letter by letter. (A scribe is permitted in MFL papers where answers are required to be given in English or Welsh.) If a candidate decides to dictate letter by letter, the dictation may be recorded and then the recording re-run to enable the candidate to spell out each word.

In MFL papers, a candidate who has approval for a scribe is able to have up to 50% extra time in place of the use of a scribe.

The word processor options and speech recognition software cannot be used in ELC, GCSE and GCE modern foreign language specifications.

Spelling, Grammar and Punctuation (SPaG) and Quality of Written Communication (QWC)
A scribe (and the various scribe options) is permitted in subjects where SPaG or QWC are being assessed. However, marks can only be awarded if the candidate has carried out the particular skills being assessed. For this reason, a candidate may sacrifice some of the SPaG marks if he does not complete these skills independently.

The candidate may choose to dictate his spellings and punctuation or to dictate just the punctuation or just the spelling, in an attempt to access some of the SPaG marks. This would be exceptionally challenging for most candidates and would need to be discussed and considered carefully, as it could impact on the quality of the candidate's responses. However, it may be appropriate for some candidates and in papers carrying marks for SPaG, a candidate who has approval for a scribe who chooses to dictate either the spellings or the punctuation or both is able to have up to 50% extra time.

25% extra time for the use of a scribe

A candidate dictating to a scribe in examinations may give rise to the need for extra time. The scribe may need the candidate to repeat his dictation or pause to allow the scribe to catch up and to read back what has been written to ensure the response has been recorded correctly.

For this reason, there is the option to add 25% extra time to an application for a scribe. The centre-based evidence (i.e. Form 8 Part 1) would outline the need for extra time for the use of the scribe but separate assessment evidence for 25% extra time in Form 8 Part 2 for this extra time is not required.

Under these circumstances, the 25% extra time is tied in with the approval for a scribe. It is not possible for the candidate to use only the extra time without the scribe. If the candidate will use 25% extra time without a scribe in any examination, this needs to be applied for separately with relevant evidence held on file that meets the criteria for 25% extra time. In the case of candidates with learning difficulties, this is likely to be assessment evidence recorded within Part 2 of Form 8.

Accommodating the use of a scribe

Candidates who use a scribe or speech recognition software in examinations are usually accommodated in a separate room so that they are not overheard and do not distract other candidates.

A scribe who is working on a one-to-one basis with a candidate who is accommodated separately can also act as the invigilator.

Language Modifier

A language modifier (LM) is a responsible adult who may clarify the carrier language in an examination paper when requested to do so by the candidate. Technical terms and subject-specific terms must not be explained or altered. An LM may also act as a reader without a separate application being required.

A LM is used for candidates who have persistent and significant difficulties with accessing and processing information. This might apply to a student with speech, language and communication needs, for example, who has difficulties understanding and processing language who may need to have the carrier language simplified or made less ambiguous. Similarly, a deaf candidate may need this arrangement to access the examination paper.

An LM is described by the JCQ as a 'rare and exceptional arrangement' and should be consider an 'arrangement of the last resort.' All other access arrangements need to be considered for the candidate and found to be unsuitable or unworkable before an LM is put in place. Other options to consider would include a reader or computer reader, extra time, and the use of a modified language paper, where available.

When making an application for a language modifier, the centre should select 'Other' on Access Arrangements Online and make a referral to the awarding body.

Training for an oral language modifier

A language modifier must either be a qualified teacher of the deaf or have undertaken accredited training and hold evidence of the training on file for JCQ centre inspection purposes. The JCQ AARA document contains the rules and a suggested memory aid for the use of a language modifier.

Accommodating the use of an language modifier

The candidate and LM will need to be accommodated in a separate room. In addition, because the use of a LM is a 'high risk' access arrangement, there must be a separate invigilator for each candidate and LM. The invigilator is required to observe the LM and listen carefully throughout the whole examination. The invigilator must then countersign the cover sheet and ensure that it accurately reflects the actions of the LM during the examination.

Practical Assistant

A practical assistant is a responsible adult who, at the instruction of the candidate, performs or assists with specifically agreed tasks during an examination. For example, a practical assistant may help with holding a ruler or turning the page.

An application is made through Access Arrangements Online and then a referral is required to the awarding body, detailing the tasks that the practical assistant will perform to ensure that the assessment objectives are not compromised by the PAs actions.

Bilingual dictionary with 10% extra time

Although the use of a bilingual translation dictionary is a centre-delegated access arrangement, 10% extra time may be permitted for the use of the dictionary if strict conditions are met. This requires evidence to be held on file and online approval. This arrangement is discussed more fully in Chapter 18.

Modified papers

Modified papers include enlarged papers, braille papers, modified language papers (where available), non-interactive PDF question papers, tactile diagrams and transcripts of listening tests and videos.

Some types of modified paper are prepared individually and, for this reason, they must be ordered by the JCQ's published deadlines.

As with all access arrangements, it is important that the candidate has had appropriate opportunities to practice using the arrangement, and this can be achieved through the use of modified past papers.

Other arrangements

The most commonly used access arrangements are listed within the JCQ Access Arrangements and Reasonable Adjustments document. However, there may be some candidates who require arrangements that are not listed. For example, a disabled candidate may be using new technology not yet covered by the regulations; a candidate with timing issues may need an individual countdown timer to keep on track; a candidate with attentional issues may require the use of ear plugs to help with concentration.

Where an arrangement is not listed on AAO, the centre should select 'Other' and make an online referral to the awarding body for the application to be considered on a case-by-case basis.

In summary....

- There are a variety of access arrangements available to candidates.
- Access arrangements reflect a candidate's current needs and normal way of working in the centre
- They are determined on an individual basis, subject by subject.
- Some access arrangements can be provided by the centre without the need for approval through Access Arrangements Online.
- Other access arrangements must be applied for, and approval gained for their use in public examinations. These arrangements require a bank of evidence to be held on file.
- Check the JCQ regulations for the evidence and approval requirements for access arrangements that you wish to put in place for candidates.

---

5. Who Can Have Access Arrangements?

Categories of need

Learners who may require examination access arrangements broadly fall into three categories:

- Those with a permanent or long-term medical condition, disability or learning difficulty
- Those who have a temporary injury or illness that arises at the time of the examination
- Those who have English as an additional language

This Guide largely deals with learners in the first category.

Chapter 18 discusses the issues around providing access arrangements for learners who have **English as an additional language**.

If a candidate who is otherwise in good health has a **temporary injury or illness that occurs at the time of the examinations**, he may require access arrangements to help to minimise the impact of the temporary condition. Provided that there is medical evidence in place to substantiate the illness or injury, the required access arrangements can be applied for through Access Arrangements Online and approval granted for one examination series. The medical evidence is then stored on file for JCQ Centre Inspection purposes.

The other measure that can be put in place for temporary occurrences is **Special Consideration**. This is a post-examination adjustment to a candidate's mark or grade to reflect temporary illness, injury or another event outside the candidate's control at the time of the examination that had, or is likely to have had, a material effect on the candidate's ability to demonstrate his normal level of attainment in an assessment. Information on the special consideration process is published in a separate JCQ document which can be accessed as an interactive document through the CAP and is also on the JCQ website.

Candidates with a long-term medical condition, disability or learning difficulty can be thought of in four broad areas of need, as set out in the SEND Code of Practice:[6]

Communication and Interaction Needs
This would include learners with speech, language and communication needs (SLCN) and those with an autism spectrum disorder (ASD).

---

[6] Department for Education and Department of Health (2015) *Special Educational Needs and Disability Code of Practice: 0 – 25 years.* Available at: https://www.gov.uk/government/publications/send-code-of-practice-0-to-25 (Accessed: 3 July 2021).

Social, Emotional and Mental Health Needs

Learners may experience a range of social and emotional difficulties and mental health conditions which manifest themselves in a variety of ways. This category would include learners with ADHD, learners with anxiety or depression and learners with eating disorders.

Sensory and Physical Needs

Learners who have a vision impairment (VI), hearing impairment (HI) or a multi-sensory impairment (MSI) would be included in this category, as would those with a physical disability (PD).

Cognition and Learning Needs

This category includes learners who have learning difficulties or specific learning difficulties (SpLD) such as dyslexia and dyscalculia.

Evidence requirements for access arrangements

The required evidence must be in place before an application can be made for the access arrangements needing approval through Access Arrangements Online. Both centre-based evidence and specialist evidence are necessary but the format of the evidence will differ according to the nature of the candidate's difficulties.

JCQ Form 8 is used for candidates with cognition and learning needs who do not have an EHCP, an IDP in Wales, or a Statement of Special Educational Needs in Northern Ireland. Part 1 is used to detail the centre-based evidence and Part 2 provides the assessment evidence.

For all other candidates, including those with:

- Communication and interaction needs
- Social, emotional and mental health needs
- Sensory and physical needs
- Cognition and learning needs who have an EHCP, IDP (Wales) or Statement of Special Educational Needs (Northern Ireland)

a file note written by the SENCO, or an equivalent member of staff in FE, is used to capture the centre-based evidence, along with accompanying specialist evidence.

Parts 2 and 3 of this Guide deal in detail with gathering and recording the centre-based evidence and specialist evidence.

The following diagram summarises the evidence requirements for each category of need:

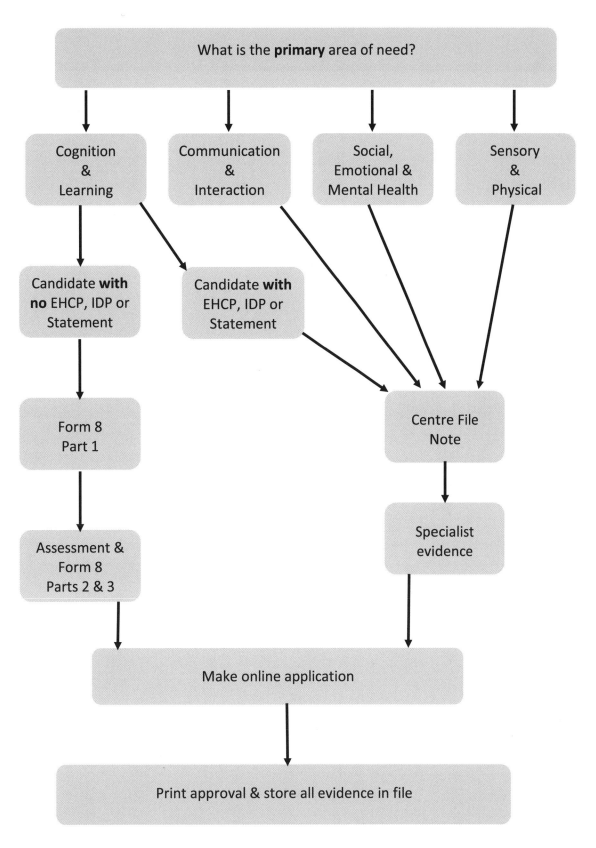

N.B. For a LM, Form 8 and assessment evidence is needed for all candidates.
For candidates with cognition and learning needs requiring more than 25% ET,
Form 8 and assessment evidence is always needed.

Part 2

The Access Arrangements Assessment

6. Gathering Centre Evidence

with contributions from Louise Green

In this chapter, the centre-based evidence that is required for access arrangements that must be approved through Access Arrangements Online will be discussed. We will consider the information that is needed, how it might be gathered, how it is recorded and by whom.

Before the centre can apply for any access arrangement requiring approval, a range of evidence to support the application is needed. The first step in compiling the evidence is gathering information in the centre. The SENCo, or the specialist assessor working in the centre, must collect centre-based information demonstrating a picture of the candidate's needs and his normal way of working within the centre. This information is vital as it contributes to the core evidence to support the request for access arrangements.

This centre-based evidence is required for all candidates. Whilst the information that is collected is the same, how it is written-up differs depending on whether an assessment is required. The previous chapter, Chapter 5, discusses the evidence requirements for each category of need. Briefly, all learners with cognition and learning needs require assessment evidence for 25% extra time or a scribe unless they have an EHCP, IDP (in Wales), or SEN Statement (in Northern Ireland). Form 8 is used for these candidates, with the centre-based information recorded in Part 1. (Later in this chapter guidance is provided for completing Form 8 Part 1). Learners with other needs, such as a physical difficulty or a sensory impairment, will not be assessed and will not have Form 8. For these candidates, the SENCo writes a file note detailing the centre-based evidence, which is accompanied by specialist evidence (see Part 3 of this Guide).

Whole-centre approach

Collecting centre-based information needs a whole-centre approach with the SENCo taking the lead on access arrangements. The SENCo works with teaching staff and support staff to gather information about the candidate. She will need to put in place systems for the candidate's subject teachers and support staff to provide her with evidence of both the candidate's difficulties and his normal way of working in lessons and when placed under timed conditions. The SENCo should ensure that the candidate is involved in this information gathering process and has the opportunity to provide details of any difficulties he experiences in his everyday study and when working under timed conditions, as well as the support strategies he finds useful.

In further education, the task of gathering centre-based information can be especially challenging, particularly in very large centres with high numbers of candidates requiring access arrangements. Effective systems need to be in place including liaison with feeder schools (for example, by email or by telephone with notes taken) and information gathering beginning at the pre-entry stage. Where limited information is available, evidence from tutors and candidates' self-reported difficulties will be particularly valuable.

The SENCo could gather information from:

- Subject teachers and course tutors
- Teaching assistants and LSAs
- Pastoral support
- Candidate
- Mentor
- Study coach
- Communication Support Worker
- Peripatetic teacher (e.g. SpLD/hearing/ vision)
- Parents (where relevant)

What evidence is needed?

The evidence that is collected will include information relating to the candidate's current needs, acquired from the start of Year 9 (for GCSE candidates) or from the start of a GCE course, as well as historical information relating to the candidate's development and earlier education.

Detailed picture of need for 25% extra time

In addition to the centre-based evidence recorded in Form 8 Part 1, the JCQ requires that supplementary evidence, known as a 'detailed picture of need' is in place for candidates with learning difficulties who require 25% extra time. The 'detailed picture of need' is the centre-based documentation that shows the need for extra time. It is stored in the candidate's evidence folder with the Form 8. During a JCQ centre inspection, the 'detailed picture of need' may be subject to scrutiny.

The supplementary evidence in the 'detailed picture of need' can come from the following sources:

Detailed picture of need – supplementary evidence

- A sample of internal school tests/mock exam papers showing the application of extra time;
- An IEP, ILP or learning plan referring to the need for extra time;
- Comments and observations from teaching staff as to why the candidate needs extra time and how he uses the extra time provided.

The amount of supplementary evidence required varies. The more robust the assessment evidence in Form 8 Part 2, the smaller the amount of supplementary evidence required in the 'detailed picture of need.'

For candidates with the standard expected assessment evidence of:

- two below average standard scores, or
- one below average standard score and one low average standard score

one piece of supplementary evidence is needed.

For candidates who do not have the standard expected assessment evidence, and where an awarding body referral will be needed, a greater amount of supplementary evidence is required, as follows:

- For two or more low average scores, two pieces of supplementary evidence are needed.
- For a cluster of at least three scores between 90 and 94 and a diagnostic report, three pieces of supplementary evidence are needed.

Centre-based evidence will also be collected for other access arrangements that are applied for using Access Arrangements Online. This will be written up on Form 8 Part 1 or the centre file note. The following pages provide examples of the documents that can contribute to the centre-based evidence.

Historical information

Background information prior to Year 9 or the GCE course could include:

- **Difficulties with literacy acquisition and development**
  Is there any evidence of difficulties in learning to read, write or spell or in maintaining progress in reading, writing and spelling as the candidate progressed through primary school and into early secondary school?

- **Sensory and Physical Needs**
  Has the candidate any medical diagnosis, poor vision, impaired hearing, delayed speech and language, communication and interaction needs, or physical disabilities that have adversely affected his progress?

- **Social, Emotional and Mental Health Needs**
  Has the candidate experienced difficulties in these areas that have adversely affected his progress? Has there been a referral to CAMHS or another mental health organisation or specialist?

- **Formal diagnosis/report**
  Is an EHCP, IDP or SEN Statement in place or are there any assessments or reports confirming the candidate's difficulties from a professional such as a specialist teacher, educational psychologist, psychiatrist, optometrist, hearing specialist, speech and language therapist or medical consultant (at specialist level, not a GP)?

- **Previous intervention strategies**

  Was any action taken in primary school or in early secondary school to support the candidate, such as differentiating the curriculum, withdrawing the candidate from parts of the curriculum, offering extra support, either 1:1 or in small groups, offering additional tuition? Were any individualised education plans (IEP) or learning support programmes (LSP) put in place for the candidate?

- **Screening tests and/or standard attainment tests**

  Do you have the results of any screening tests and/or standard attainment tests from primary school and early secondary school?

- **Previous access arrangements**

  Has the candidate ever been given access arrangements in previous situations such as National Curriculum Tests (SATs), music exams or drama exams, or GCSEs if the candidate is now taking GCEs?

Examples of sources of historical information	
Data from baseline assessments	This could be taken from the results of whole year group baseline assessments such as CATs, Yellis and MidYIS. Discrepancies between scores might suggest a specific learning difficulty.
Pupil tracking data	School data is used to track and monitor progress and might be used as evidence if the candidate falls behind expectations. If this happens it also can trigger support with targeted interventions.
Information from parents	Parents may be able to confirm if there is a family history of specific learning difficulties or they may be able to provide a copy of a letter from a medical consultant or another professional confirming the candidate's difficulty.
Previous assessments	Previous assessments can provide evidence of the candidate's persistent and significant difficulties.
Historical school reports	Teacher comments in school reports may highlight where the candidate is having difficulty in the classroom.
Previous differentiation/support in class	An educational support plan such as EHCP, ILP or ESP will highlight the candidate's historical difficulties and inform the SENCo of the support that has been offered in the classroom. Information reported by previous teachers and/or support staff can also be used if this is available.

Current Information

To accompany the historical data, the SENCo must gather information relating to the candidate's current studies, as follows:

Current needs

Information detailing the candidate's current difficulties when working in the classroom and when placed under timed conditions in tests and examinations.

Such difficulties might include:

- Difficulties with reading accurately
- Difficulties understanding text-based information
- Needing help with writing or spelling
- Poor, slow and/or illegible handwriting
- Not writing in sufficient detail
- Difficulty planning work and/or thinking of what to write
- Not answering the exact question asked
- Poor memory for instructions
- Difficulty following instructions
- Poor organisational skills
- Behavioural difficulties
- Maintaining focus/concentration
- Slow speed of work, e.g. reading, writing, transferring ideas to paper
- Taking longer than expected with tasks set in class
- Running out of time in class tests and school exams

Current intervention strategies

Information detailing any support and differentiation that is currently in place for the candidate in the classroom.

Adjustments might include:

- Support for reading, writing or understanding from a teaching assistant or LSA
- Asking other learners for support on a regular basis
- Having to read work aloud or the use of a reading pen
- Instructions broken down or written guidelines provided
- Differentiated work to take account of a difficulty (e.g. slow speed of working)
- The provision of handouts or outline notes
- Lists of key words and subject-specific words to support spelling and vocabulary
- Writing frames and templates to support writing
- The use of a word processor for writing tasks
- Coloured paper or enlarged font

Arrangements made for internal school exams/mock examinations

Information detailing arrangements that are already in place, or that will be put in place when appropriate, to support the candidate in tests and examinations, including mock exams. Access arrangements could include 25% extra time and methods for supporting reading, spelling or writing.

Possible sources of current information	
Information reported by subject teachers and/ or support staff	The SENCo can use emails, electronic or paper questionnaires and checklists to elicit information. (See below)
Candidate's self-reported difficulties	A structured interview is a useful way to gather information from the candidate about any difficulties he experiences in his everyday study and when working under timed conditions, as well as the support strategies he finds useful.
Information from parents	Where appropriate, comments from parents about how the candidate works at home, such as time taken to complete homework and any difficulties encountered when working at home with reading, writing and completing work.
Current school or college reports	Comments from school reports may add to the picture of need and confirm normal way of working in different subjects.
Current Individual Learning Plan/Education Support Plans	A current ILP/ESP may outline the candidate's needs and include details of support that is in place.
EHCP, IDP or SEN Statements	Information contained in a current EHCP, IDP or SEN Statement may contribute useful information for the SENCo's file note.
Arrangements made for internal school exams/mock examinations	Teachers can provide the SENCo with information about the support in place for class tests. The SENCo should liaise with the Exams Officer to confirm the support in place, or that will be put in place, when the candidate takes any mock exams.

Gathering information from teaching staff and support staff

Carefully designed emails, electronic or paper questionnaires and checklists can help busy teachers and support staff to provide useful and relevant information in an efficient way. The following pages contain examples of documents that can be used for this purpose. These, and other useful forms, are available for purchasers of this Guide to download from the Patoss website (see Appendix 2).

Below is an example of a checklist requesting information on the candidate's difficulties in the classroom that could be sent to teachers and support staff.

Name of Student:	Name of Teacher/Tutor:		
Course:	Year Group:		

TIME		YES	NO
Finishes tasks after others			
Needs extra time for assignments			
Needs time to formulate an answer to a verbal question (slow responding)			
Needs careful explanations in straightforward language of tasks/assignment titles			
READING		YES	NO
Needs reading support in class			
Avoids reading out loud			
Has difficulty following written instructions			
Finds it difficult to quickly get the idea of what s/he has read			
Finds it hard to remember what s/he has read			
WRITTEN WORK		YES	NO
Handwriting is difficult to read			
Has difficulty copying from the board			
Finds taking notes hard			
Works on laptop/computer rather than writing by hand			
Needs support with planning written work			
Can explain verbally without problems but struggles to write anything down			
Needs support with spelling			
Grammar and punctuation insecure			
MEMORY & CONCENTRATION		YES	NO
Has difficulty following oral instructions			
Has difficulty concentrating for long periods			
Has difficulty remembering messages, appointments			
Needs to have instructions repeated			
Needs to have instructions written down			

PRACTICAL TASKS	YES	NO
Prefers practical tasks to written ones		
Understanding is better if able to consolidate learning through practical experience		

ORGANISATION	YES	NO
Organisational skills are weak – loses things, forgets items s/he needs to bring		
Finds it hard to meet deadlines		
Has difficulty working efficiently		

VISION	YES	NO
Needs large print version		
Uses coloured overlay when reading. **Please state colour:**		
Benefits from handouts on coloured paper. **Please state colour:**		

EXAMS	YES	NO
Finds revising for exams hard		
Unable to finish an exam in the time allowed		
Panics when faced with tests		
Needs to take frequent rest breaks		
Needs timely reminders to stay focused on task		

Any other information

What adjustments are made in lessons, tests or exams?

Date normal way of working discussed and agreed:

Tutor Signature:

Student signature:

Patoss: This sheet can be photocopied without infringing copyright

Electronic methods of collecting data

Emails and online forms and questionnaires can be a time-efficient way of collecting feedback from teachers and support staff.

Below is an example of an email asking teachers and support staff for information on the candidate's difficulties in the classroom and the support strategies that are used.

You are receiving this communication because you teach (put subject here) to: (put student's name and year group here)

Please could you name at least **one area** where (student's name) struggles in class?

Please could you give **two ways** in which you are helping (student's name) in class/outside the classroom?

Thank you

Online data collecting sites

Forms for staff to complete can be compiled using online data collection sites. There are many sites, both free and subscription-based (e.g. e.g. Google Docs, Survey Monkey, Office 365, iSAMS) where the information is only shared between the sender and the recipient(s). Using data collections sites can be useful as these collate the information and display it in a variety of formats (e.g. pie charts, bar charts, spreadsheets). It is easy to check which members of staff have responded and email reminders can be sent via the system if staff are slow to respond. The following pages contains two example of forms that could be created online and used to collect evidence for extra time. They could be adapted to collect evidence of the need for a scribe.[7]

---

[7] Adapted from examples created by G. Cadman, Dr Challoner's Grammar School, Amersham.

Evidence Collection for Extra Time – Online Form 1

Please remember, your professional judgement is valid, and there is no right or wrong answer. If you have any questions or concerns, please contact SENCo.

1. Subject taught ………………………………………………………

2. Does this student show evidence of need for extra time in class tests/exams in your subject? *Mark only one box.*

	Yes
	No *Skip to question 7*

Evidence from class tests/exams

3. Please give an example of a class test or exam in your subject where this student showed evidence of need for more time.

4. Please select the reason(s) this student needed the extra time. (Select all that apply)

	Test/exam not finished
	Large gaps where questions were missed out
	Work not properly checked
	Work not proof-read
	Work done hastily/rushed
	Other (please specify)

5. What was done to compensate for this student on this occasion? (Select all that apply)

	Extra time given immediately afterwards
	Additional time given at lunch break
	Test/exam taken home to complete
	Mark adjusted to reflect progress
	Other (please specify)

6. Does this example reflect the student's regular and normal way of working in exams/class tests in your subject? *Mark only one box.*

	Yes
	No

7. Does this student show evidence of need for extra time in class work in your lessons? *Mark only one box.*

	Yes
	No *Skip to question 12*

Extra time in lessons

8. Please give an example from lessons and class work in your subjects where this student showed evidence of need for more time.

| |
| |

9. Please select the reason this student needed the extra time. (Select all that apply)

	Not able to finish reading task
	Needed to re-read material to process meaning
	Unfinished note-taking during given time
	Uncompleted activities set in class
	Less work done in comparison to peers in class
	Work rushed/done too hastily
	Unable to remember instructions
	Needed re-explanation
	Unable to maintain concentration
	Other (please specify)

10. What was done to compensate for this student on this occasion? (Select all that apply)

	Work completed at lunch/break
	Work completed at home
	Notes copied from a friend
	Photo of notes taken on iPad
	Additional time given in class
	Instructions repeated or written guidelines provided
	Rest breaks
	Other (please specify)

11. Does this example reflect the student's regular and normal way of working in your lessons? *Mark only one box.*

| | Yes |
| | No   *Go to question 12* |

12. Any other relevant information:

| |
| |

Evidence Collection for Extra Time – Online Form 2

The main heading to set up this online survey are:

- Time stamp

- Email address

- Subject taught

- Does this student show evidence of need for 25% extra time?

- Do any of the following issues apply to this student?
  - Works slowly in class
  - Does not produce enough work
  - Does not give enough detail in their answer
  - Loses marks as they have misread the question
  - Loses marks as they have made errors which they could have spotted if they had checked their work
  - Has difficulty remembering instructions
  - Has difficulty following instructions

- What is the student's history of difficulty in your subject?

- What are the student's current difficulties in tests and examinations?

- What support and adjustments are in place in tests and exams in your subject?

- What are the student's current difficulties in classroom learning?

- What support and adjustments are in place for the candidate in the classroom in your subject?

- Any other relevant information?

Methods of referral

Subject teachers should be encouraged to raise any concerns they may have about candidates at the earliest opportunity. These can then be followed up by the SENCo and, where appropriate, support, adjustments and access arrangements can be put in place.

Questionnaires can be a useful way for teachers to refer their concerns to the SENCo as they provide a written (or electronic) record which can contribute to the picture of need for access arrangements. All teaching staff need to be made aware of the system that is used for referrals, so that the procedures are universally adopted. Forms need to be easily accessible and user-friendly so that the referral process is not perceived to be excessively onerous. They could be kept in the staffroom or, electronically, on a staff intranet.

Questionnaires can also be used to encourage teachers and support staff to identify potential candidates for access arrangements who are struggling but have not yet been recognised as having learning needs that will require adjustments. An example of a form is shown below:

Please list any students in your teaching groups whose performance in written work / timed tests / recent end of year exams / mock examinations did not match your expectations.			
Name of Student	Year Group	Reason(s) for concern: *e.g. panic, lack of time, lack of preparation, misreading questions, mis-answering questions, poor exam technique*	Suggestions to help in future and/or adjustments that could be made

The next page provides an example of a referral form that could be used in hard copy or electronic format. This form, and the form above, can be downloaded from the Patoss website (see Appendix 2).

Referral Form

Please complete this form if you have concerns over a student who does not appear to be making the expected progress.

Name of teacher and subject:		Name of student:	

	Yes	No
Has difficulty maintaining focus		
Reading appears to be a problem		
Appears to read more slowly than others		
Appears to write more slowly than others		
Writing is generally illegible, even when taking care		
Does not appear to be able to listen and take notes at the same time		
Oral work is much better than written work		
Tends to be disorganised		
Assignments are often handed in late (or not at all)		
Does not appear able to plan work		
Work lacks structure		
Spelling is a problem		
Grammar and punctuation are insecure		
Reluctant to participate in group and class discussions		
Recent exam result did not meet expectation		

Other comments, including specific examples:

Samples of work attached	Yes	No	Samples of work available	Yes	No

Signed: Date:

Patoss: This sheet can be photocopied without infringing copyright

Information from the candidate

For candidates who have difficulties that are known to centre staff, the SENCo can conduct a structured interview to gather information for support, including access arrangements.

Candidates should also be encouraged to inform teaching staff as early as possible if they have difficulties in class or have had previous difficulties during exams (for example when a candidate moves from a school to a further education college).

Below is an example of a checklist that could be completed by the candidate (or as part of a structured interview) to provide information on how he sees his difficulties in the classroom. This form 'Student's view of Normal Way of Working' can be downloaded from the Patoss website (see Appendix 2).

Name of Student:	Name of Teacher/Tutor:		
Course:	Year Group:		
TIME		YES	NO
I finish tasks after others			
I need extra time for assignments			
I need to take time to think before I can answer a question			
I need the teacher to explain a task again before I understand what to do			
READING		YES	NO
I have a computer for reading support or someone to read to me in class			
I dislike reading out loud			
Reading out loud helps me to understand what I read			
I find it hard to follow written instructions			
I often do not understand what I have just read			
I find it hard to remember what I have read			
WRITTEN WORK		YES	NO
My handwriting is hard to read for me and/or for others			
I have difficulty copying from the board			
I find it hard to take notes			
I work better when typing than writing by hand			
I need help to plan my written work			
I can talk through my answers, but I find it hard to write anything down			
I need help with spelling			
I am not good at grammar and punctuation			

MEMORY & CONCENTRATION	YES	NO
I have difficulty following what the teacher says		
I have difficulty concentrating for long periods		
I have difficulty remembering messages, appointments		
I need to have instructions repeated		
I need to have instructions written down		
PRACTICAL TASKS	YES	NO
I find practical tasks hard		
I prefer practical tasks to written ones		
I understand better if I can do an activity rather than listening/writing about it		
ORGANISATION	YES	NO
I am not well-organised – I lose things and forget to bring items to school		
I find it hard to meet deadlines		
I have difficulty working efficiently		
VISION	YES	NO
I need a large print version of handouts		
I use a coloured overlay when reading. The colour I use is:		
The print blurs or shimmers on the page		
I prefer handouts on coloured paper. The colour I prefer is:		
EXAMS	YES	NO
I find it hard to revise for exams		
I cannot finish an exam in the time allowed		
I often go blank in tests and exams		
I need to take frequent rest breaks		
I need to be reminded to stay focused on task		

What do teachers do to help you in your lessons, tests and exams?
What do you do to help yourself in your lessons, tests and exams?
Any other information
Date normal way of working discussed:
Student signature: **Learning Support signature:**

Patoss: This sheet can be photocopied without infringing copyright

Change of pen colour

A useful method of assessing speed of working is to ask the candidate to use a different coloured pen, for example:

- for finishing work at home that the teacher expected to be completed in the lesson.
- for homework when the recommended time set for that particular task has elapsed.
- for extra time given in tests and examinations.

The candidate's work or exam papers showing a change of pen colour can form part of the centre-based evidence that is used to support an application for access arrangements.

Feedback from examinations

Staff involved in overseeing and invigilating tests and examinations can provide useful feedback for the SENCo on how candidates used their access arrangements, and for the examinations officer on administrative concerns such as room signage and lighting. A feedback form can be a convenient way to capture this information. An example of a form that can be used for this purpose is shown on the next page.[8] This form 'Staff Feedback Access Arrangements' can be downloaded from the Patoss website (see Appendix 2).

Following mock examinations, the SENCo can conduct meetings with candidates to review the use of their particular access arrangements to ensure they are useful and appropriate.

Storing information

Once the centre-based evidence has been collected, the SENCo will use summarise the information on Form 8 Part 1 or a Centre File Note. It will also form the supplementary evidence for the 'detailed picture of need for 25% extra time for candidates with learning difficulties' (see page 58). The SENCo then stores the evidence either as paper copies or electronically. Evidence of need must be available in the centre for inspection for all candidates with an approved access arrangement. See Chapter 16 for information on the storage of evidence and the JCQ Centre Inspection.

---

[8] From an idea suggested by Roger Lewis, SpLD Base Team Leader, Francis Combe School and Community College, Watford, Herts.

Staff Feedback – Access Arrangements

Please complete this form after each exam during which you have supported a candidate with access arrangements and return it as soon as possible to ....

Your comments will help us to support the student effectively and deal with any administrative shortcomings in future exam sessions.

Student	Date
Exam	End of year exam Mock Public exam Other (specify)

The student was allowed:
    25% extra time
    Exam reading pen
    Computer reader
    Reader
    Word processor
    Speech recognition software
    Scribe
    Bilingual dictionary
    Prompter
    Practical assistant
    Other (specify)
	S/he used the arrangement
	    Fully
	    Frequently
	    Infrequently
	    Not at all
	
	S/he appeared
	    Calm & on task
	    Anxious
	    Other (specify)

Any comments/suggestions regarding future exam arrangements for this student? Any other comments? E.g. implications for revision.	
Room number	Did you have all the information & resources you needed?

The room was
    Quiet / Mostly quiet / noisy
    Well-lit / Poorly lit
    Too hot / Too cold / Stuffy
    Other (specify)
	Guidance sheets
	    Cover sheet
	    Spare equipment
	    Signs for doors and corridors
	    Other (specify)

Any other comments/suggestions	
Your name	

Patoss: This sheet can be photocopied without infringing copyright

Candidates working outside the centre, including private candidates

Learners may be working remotely outside the centre for a variety of reasons, for example:

- a private candidate who is home-educated and using the centre for examinations;
- a learner who has left the school or college and is returning to retake exams;
- a learner studying on a part-time college course which involves home study;
- in periods of school or college closure where learning is delivered remotely, such as during the Covid-19 pandemic.

Online applications for access arrangements must always be substantiated with the required evidence, including centre-based evidence of need and normal way of working. Therefore the SENCo must gather this information for candidates working outside the centre who require access arrangements in examinations they take in the centre.

Support methods may differ when a learner is working outside the centre. Parents or partners may play a role in supporting learning and there may be an increased use of assistive technology. It can be challenging to obtain information for learners working outside the centre, particularly when they are not known to teaching staff or the SENCo. The chart contains some ideas to consider for gathering information.

Work Log	Ask the candidate to keep a log of their working methods for assignments, for example, support from another individual or use of technology, and the time taken to complete the work. The work log can provide useful evidence about the candidate's needs and normal way of working.
Past paper - **in centre, or** - **using a video link**	The candidate completes a past paper or subject test at home via a video link, or comes into the centre to do so. This will enable the access arrangements to be observed in progress. The completed paper can be kept on file with a note of the access arrangements that were used.
Screening tests - **in centre, or** - **using a video link**	The candidate comes into centre to complete screening tests, or the tests are administered remotely via a video link. Computer-based screening tests will be particularly useful. The results can inform a support plan as well as providing objective evidence for access arrangements that can be recorded in Form 8 Part 1.
Feedback about normal way of working	Feedback can be provided by the candidate, parents, and any teachers familiar with the candidate. Questionnaires can be created or adapted and a structured interview could be conducted by telephone or video link. Examples of the candidate's work could be kept on file alongside the feedback.

Reporting the centre-based information

Once the centre-based information has been gathered, the SENCo must complete paperwork to encapsulate the evidence. There are two methods of reporting the information:

- **A Centre File Note** is used for candidates who have

    o Communication and interaction needs
    o Sensory and physical needs
    o Social, emotional and mental health needs
    o An Education, Health and Care Plan (EHCP), IDP (Wales) or Statement of Special Educational Needs (Northern Ireland)

    Part 3 of this Guide provides information on the Centre File Note and its accompanying specialist evidence.

- **A Form 8 'report'** is, in effect, a profile of learning difficulties for candidates with cognition and learning needs who do not have an EHCP, IDP or SEN Statement. It includes:

    o Part 1 – the history of difficulties and current needs, completed by the SENCo or in-house assessor
    o Part 2 – the standardised scores, completed by the assessor.
    o Part 3 – the arrangements that are being applied for, completed by the SENCo with the Declaration signed by the SENCo or equivalent member of staff or the Head of Centre.

The table on the next page shows the various methods to record centre-based evidence of need and normal way of working. The first column shows the method used to record the evidence; the second column shows the access arrangements and the third column shows the types of candidates the method is used for.

Remember, most arrangements listed below require specialist evidence (e.g. assessment evidence in Form 8 Part 2; a letter/report from a medical consultant) alongside the centre-based evidence.

Pages 78 and 79 provide information to help with completing Form 8 Part 1.

A guidance sheet for the completion of the whole of Form 8 is available on the Patoss website as a downloadable resource (see Appendix 2).

Method of recording centre evidence	Access Arrangements	Categories of candidates
Short concise file note	• Supervised Rest Breaks • Reader/Computer Reader	All candidates
Form 8 Part 1	• Scribe • 25% Extra Time	Candidates with learning difficulties (without EHCP, IDP or SEN Statement)
	• Extra time of up to 50% (between 26% to 50% extra time)	All candidates with learning difficulties (including those with an EHCP, IDP or SEN Statement)
	• Language modifier	All candidates
Detailed File Note	• Scribe • 25% Extra Time	Candidates with Communication & Interaction, Sensory & Physical, SEMH needs and candidates with EHCP, IDP or SEN Statement for learning difficulties
	• Extra time of up to 50% (between 26% to 50% extra time	Candidates with Communication & Interaction, Sensory & Physical, SEMH needs
	• Extra time of over 50%	All candidates (not available for learning difficulties)
Centre documentation showing JCQ criteria (AARA 5.18.6) has been met	• Bilingual Dictionary with 10% extra time	EAL candidates who meet JCQ criteria in AARA 5.18

Completing Form 8 Part 1

The SENCO (or FE equivalent), or assessor working within the centre, completes Part 1 before the candidate is assessed.

Part 1 – answer the three key statements

What is the candidate's history of difficulties?

Provide relevant information/evidence of the candidate's persistent and significant difficulties, the history of difficulties. For example

- Does the candidate have a formal diagnosis/existing report (e.g. dyslexia/dyspraxia)? If yes, summarise briefly
- Have screening tests, CAT tests been carried out? If yes, summarise briefly
- What is known about their difficulties with literacy acquisition and development?
- What support was offered at primary/previous school/s or earlier in the current centre?
- What difficulties are noted on their ILP, if they have one?
- What historic difficulties does the candidate report? (e.g. taking longer than others to complete work, poor memory, difficulties with understanding what is read, poor spelling.)

What are the candidate's current difficulties in the classroom, tests and examinations?

Detail the current difficulties to show how they have impacted on teaching and learning and performance in exams. Provide evidence of feedback from teachers and/or support staff.

- What difficulties have the candidate/ teachers / tutors / support staff reported?
  (N.B. The areas of difficulty may vary by subject area so you should report feedback from teaching staff to explain difficulties in subjects with different requirements, for example, maths and English, if they are different.)
- How do these difficulties impact on the candidate's learning?
  (e.g. difficulty getting thoughts down on paper; written work does not reflect subject knowledge; cannot fully access the curriculum through printed material; does not complete work within the allotted time.)

What support and adjustments are in place for the candidate in the classroom, tests and examinations?

Detail the normal way of working, the support given and how this relates to the proposed arrangement(s). For example, have teaching staff recorded any support regularly provided in the classroom?

- What support is given/what reasonable adjustments or access arrangements are made in the classroom, tests and exams?
  (e.g. Teaching Assistant/LSA support, assistive technology, candidate placed in a small class, extended deadlines, extra time in tests and exams, attends catch up classes, attends study skills classes, is on a reduced timetable/curriculum)
- Do the adjustments made vary depending on the subject area? If yes, explain how (e.g. candidate uses a word processor, prompt and extra time in English **but** in Maths they use a human reader who acts as prompt and they work quickly so extra time is not required).

Part 1

Any other relevant information

Provide any other relevant information
- Is English an additional language?
- Have the candidate's difficulties only just come to light?
  (This might help explain why the history of difficulties might not be extensive.)
- Does the candidate have any co-occurring difficulties in addition to the learning difficulties outlined?
  (Extra time or a scribe: the learning difficulties are the principal difficulty, but there are secondary issues within the learner's profile.
  Language modifier: Form 8 is used for all learners requiring a LM, so a hearing impairment or autism may be the principal category of need.)
- Is the learner home-educated or have there been extensive periods of home study?

In summary...

- The SENCo takes the lead on access arrangements.
- There must be a whole centre approach, with effective communication between the SENCO and staff members.
- Teachers and support staff need to provide the SENCO with evidence of the learner's difficulties and his normal way of working.
- Forms and questionnaires can be used to gather information.
- Information can be stored in hard copy or electronic format.
- A picture of need and normal way of working is needed for all candidates (including private candidates taking their exams in the centre) when an access arrangement is applied for using Access Arrangements Online.
- The centre-based information is captured on Form 8 Part 1 or on a Centre File Note.
- The SENCo must complete Part 1 of Form 8 before the assessment can take place.

7. The Access Arrangements Assessment

The remaining chapters in Part 2 deal with the assessment evidence that is needed to accompany the centre-based evidence. Candidates who have cognition and learning needs (and in some cases, who do not have a current EHCP or IDP in Wales or SEN Statement in Northern Ireland) require assessment evidence for certain access arrangements. All candidates require assessment evidence for a language modifier. The access arrangements assessment will be discussed in detail, including who is able to carry out the assessment, test choices and the access arrangements assessment report.

Part 3 of this Guide will look at the specialist evidence that is needed for learners who do not require assessment evidence for certain arrangements, including those with communication and interaction needs, sensory and physical needs and social, emotional and mental health needs and all learners with an EHCP, IPD (Wales) or SEN Statement (Northern Ireland).

Who can assess for access arrangements?

Assessors who can conduct access arrangements assessments fall into three categories:

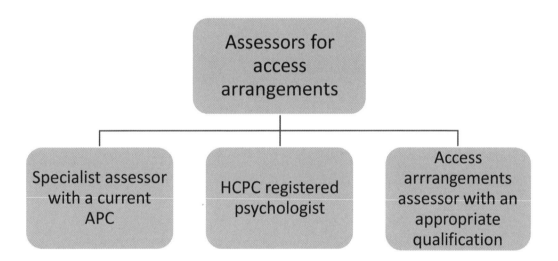

- **A specialist assessor holding a current SpLD Assessment Practising Certificate (APC)** as awarded by Patoss, the Dyslexia Guild or the British Dyslexia Association. APC holders are listed on the SpLD Assessment Standards Committee (SASC) website.[9] The website shows the date that the APC was first awarded and the expiry date by which it needs to be renewed in order to stay current.

  APC holders are specialist teachers who have undergone postgraduate training in both specialist teaching and assessment. They are suitably qualified to carry out

---

[9] APC holders are listed in the 'Assessors' section of the SASC website: https://sasc.org.uk/Assessors.aspx

diagnostic assessments for specific learning difficulties as well as access arrangements assessments.

A screenshot of the specialist assessor's listing on the SASC website or a copy of the APC certificate, current at the time of the assessment, can be used to evidence the assessor's qualification.

- **An appropriately qualified psychologist registered with the Health and Care Professions Council** will be included in the HCPC Register. The register contains the name and location of the practitioner, as well as their registration number and the date of registration. It is located on the HCPC website.[10]

  HCPC registered psychologists have undergone extensive training and are able to carry out diagnostic assessments and access arrangements assessments. In addition to the assessment tools that are available for use by appropriately trained teacher-assessors, HCPC registered psychologists have access to some 'closed' tests that cannot be used by other assessors.

  A screenshot of the psychologist's registration on the HCPC website can be used to evidence the assessor's qualification.

- **An access arrangements assessor** is a specially trained practitioner who has successfully completed a postgraduate course at, or equivalent to, Level 7, including at least 100 hours relating to individual specialist assessment.

  Within the training course, the '100 hours' will incorporate lecture, seminar and tutorial time. Time spent in private study and completing course assignments is also included, as are any assessments that are undertaken as part of the coursework requirements.

  The JCQ stipulates the areas that access arrangements assessor training courses must cover. These encompass a broad understanding of psychometrics, the selection and use of standardised tests and the ethical issues involved in testing.

  Courses that are accredited at APC or AMBDA level fulfil the JCQ criteria for access arrangements assessor training. Assessors who have a qualification at this level (usually a postgraduate diploma in specialist assessment) are able to carry out both access arrangements assessments and diagnostic assessments.

  In addition, a postgraduate course at, or equivalent to, Level 7 that provides a qualification in access arrangements assessments such as the **Patoss AAA: Assessing**

---

[10] The HCPC Register is located on the website: http://www.hpc-uk.org/check/

for **Access Arrangements** course, fulfils the JCQ criteria.[11] Assessors who hold a 'standalone' qualification in access arrangements assessment can carry out such assessments but will need to refer a learner to another professional if a diagnostic assessment is required.

A copy of the course certificate can be used to evidence the assessor's qualification. In addition, AAA certificate holders are listed on the Patoss website and PAPAA certificate holders are listed on the Include-ed website. A screenshot of the website listing can provide evidence of the assessor's qualification in access arrangements assessment.[12]

Requirements for all assessors

In addition to their qualification in assessment, all assessors who conduct assessments for access arrangements must be either a HCPC registered psychologist or hold an appropriate qualification to teach and make recommendations for secondary-aged or adult learners with learning difficulties. This might, for example, be Qualified Teacher Status (QTS), a PGCE qualification or a further education teaching qualification. A specialist teaching qualification in teaching and supporting learners with specific learning difficulties/dyslexia, such as a Level 5 diploma, also fulfils this requirement.

All assessors will need to have an in-depth and up-to-date understanding of the JCQ regulations, must appreciate the principles, procedures and accountabilities involved in access arrangements and be familiar with the Equality Act 2010, such that they can help to identify access arrangements that might assist the candidate in exams and assessments.

In-house Assessor

To ensure that the access arrangements process is joined-up, the assessor will liaise with the SENCo and obtain Part 1 before testing takes place so that the assessment takes account of the centre-based evidence. Following the assessment, the assessor will feedback the results to the SENCo, including discussing any information that has come to light during the assessment that may be relevant in determining appropriate access arrangements. The one-to-one assessment environment can sometimes lead to a learner revealing difficulties or strategies that may not have been picked up previously, such as taking much longer than expected to complete homework, or a useful support or revision strategy. For this reason, it is preferable that the assessor is employed within the centre.

---

[11]Communicate-Ed's PAPAA, Real Training's CPT3A and Education Elephant's ETAAC are examples of other courses providing a qualification in assessing for access arrangements.

[12] Patoss AAA certificate holders are listed on the Patoss website: https://www.patoss-dyslexia.org/AAA-Certificate-Holders; PAPAA graduates are listed on the Include-ed website: https://www.include-ed.org.uk/papaa-course/graduates/

In some settings, the SENCo is also the access arrangements assessor and is responsible for gathering both the centre-based evidence and the assessment evidence. Alternatively, the assessor could be another member of the teaching staff who holds an appropriate assessment qualification.

Some centres contract the services of an assessor who comes into the centre specifically to carry out assessments. Such an assessor may work for a number of schools and colleges and be paid directly by each one, making them the in-house assessor for each centre.

An educational psychologist or specialist assessor employed by the Local Authority works under contract to the centre and is able to carry out access arrangements assessments for candidates on that basis as an in-house assessor.

External Assessor

An assessor who is not employed within, or contracted by, the centre is an external assessor (sometimes known as an independent assessor). It is possible for an external assessor to carry out access arrangements assessments provided that the process is followed correctly. The external assessor must have an 'established working relationship' with the centre and must be approved by the head of the centre. This means that before any assessment can take place, the external assessor provides the centre with evidence of her qualification and the centre agrees to accept assessment evidence from the assessor.

Prior to the assessment, the assessor liaises with the SENCo who provides her with the centre-based evidence. The order of the process must be strictly adhered to so that there is a basis for the assessment that originates from the centre. Even if there is not a great deal of centre-based evidence before an assessment takes place, an outline or 'skeleton' Form 8 Part 1 must be provided to the assessor as a minimum.

Privately Commissioned Assessments

An assessment that takes place without any prior consultation with the centre cannot be used as assessment evidence for access arrangements. It is crucial, therefore, that learners and their parents do not engage the services of an independent assessor who has no working relationship with the centre with the expectation that the results can be used for access arrangements in examinations at the centre.

It is important to help parents to understand the access arrangements process and the procedures that must be followed so that potential conflicts can be averted and expectations can be managed. This can be achieved by:

- A system in place in the centre to address parental concerns about learners' progress and support, including access arrangements. Parents who feel that their concerns are listened to and dealt with should have less reason to seek an independent assessment.

- The centre producing clear guidance for parents setting out how the access arrangements process works in their setting and who to contact for more information. Parents might be provided with a leaflet at the start of GCSE or GCE courses or directed to information published on the centre's website.

- Independent assessors or psychologists who undertake private assessment work for learners in secondary or further education having a good understanding of the access arrangements process and regulations and ensuring that they work ethically when their services are contracted. The assessor should explain to a parent seeking an assessment that any results cannot be used for access arrangements unless the centre provides the assessor with centre-based information (Form 8 Part 1) prior to the assessment and agrees to accept the assessor's qualification evidence and report (Form 8 Part 2).

See the next page for an example of information useful to include in a leaflet or guidance sheet for parents and students.

Despite it not being able to be used for access arrangements, if a privately-commissioned report comes into the centre, it should not simply be dismissed as it may provide worthwhile information about the learner's support needs. On occasion, a learner who has genuine needs may 'slip under the radar' in the centre and the report may highlight issues that have gone hitherto unnoticed. In such a scenario, the process of gathering centre-based information and assessing the candidate in the centre should be put in place. Relevant information from the private report can be included in Part 1 of Form 8.

In summary...

- Those who carry out assessments for access arrangements must be suitably qualified, meeting the JCQ criteria for an assessor.
- Assessors can evidence their qualification(s) using a screenshot from a website or by providing the centre with a copy of their qualification certificate.
- Preferably, the assessor will work within the centre.
- Assessors working independently of the centre must be accepted by the centre and liaise with the centre.
- Assessment reports from independent assessors who have carried out an assessment without prior consultation with the centre cannot be accepted.
- Centres should ensure that learners and parents are informed about the assessment process within the centre.

Access Arrangements - Information for students and parents

Access arrangements are 'reasonable adjustments' for students who have a disability or a special educational need that significantly affects them in exams.

Access arrangements
- Do not change the skills or knowledge being tested
- Must not give an unfair advantage, but...
- Do give a level playing field so students can show their knowledge

There are a variety of access arrangements that can be provided, including:
- Support for reading (e.g. a reader, text-to-speech software, a reading pen)
- Support for writing (e.g. a scribe, speech-to-text software, a word processor)
- Support for working to time (e.g. 25% extra time, rest breaks)

Any arrangements that are used in exams are based on the normal way of working in the classroom and in tests and exams. Wherever possible, access arrangements that enable a student to work independently are encouraged.

Evidence is needed for some access arrangements and these need to be applied for and approved before they can be used in external exams. This sometimes means that testing needs to be carried out. Testing takes place in *school/college*. Strict rules must be followed so that the test scores can be used as evidence for access arrangements.

Please note: assessments that have been carried out without prior contact with the *school/college* cannot be used for access arrangements.

We will always seek to work with students and parents to ensure the most appropriate outcome for all students.

Please contact [*name and role within school/college*] if you have any concerns and we will be happy to advise.

Ethical and Objective Assessment

It is important to consider the ethical administration of access arrangements assessments. Assessors must work with professional integrity to conduct impartial assessments and gain fair results which will be part of the evidence base for access arrangements.

The JCQ AARA document sets out the accountabilities of those involved in the access arrangements process, including the assessor.

The assessor must:

> - Record the results of any tests completed indicating that the impairment has a substantial and long-term adverse effect on the candidate's performance.

You will notice that this point links with the language of the Equality Act 2010. It is, essentially, saying that the assessor must report within Form 8 Part 2 those assessment results that indicate a significant difficulty or disability.

> - Work only within their area of expertise and in an ethical fashion.

Assessors must understand what their qualifications enable them to do, be aware of the limitations of their skills and experience and be able to determine when it is necessary to refer a candidate to another professional.

> - Use age-appropriate, nationally standardised and up-to-date tests appropriate to the individual.

This point will be covered in Chapter 8. The assessor must select tests that will provide robust, relevant and reliable assessment evidence.

> - Report the results of their assessment within Part 2 of Form 8.

The use of JCQ Form 8 Part 2 ensures that assessment data is reported in a consistent way across centres, making the process clearer and helping the JCQ Centre Inspector to ascertain that the required supporting evidence is in place.

> - Provide the centre with evidence of their qualification(s) before assessing any candidate.

It is essential for the centre to know, and be able to demonstrate, that all assessors conducting access arrangements assessments for candidates in the centre are suitably qualified to undertake this work. This maintains the integrity of the assessment evidence and, indeed, the whole access arrangements process.

The simplest way for an assessor to provide the centre with evidence of her qualification(s) is by giving a copy of the qualification certificate. Alternatively, a screenshot of a listing on a relevant website could be printed out and stored.

The Patoss Code of Ethics

Patoss requires its members to follow its Code of Ethics and Conduct. An important precept of the Code is to encourage confidence on the part of members and the public in the standards of practice which Patoss supports. The full Code of Ethics can be found on the Patoss website.[13]

Whilst assessors who conduct access arrangements assessments are not required to be members of Patoss, the principles of the Code of Ethics set out below are relevant to the work of all assessors, including those who conduct access arrangements assessments.

Competence and Quality of Practice

- **Only undertake work for which they are suitably qualified and experienced**
  As already discussed, it is essential for the assessor to know what she can do, what she cannot do and when another professional is needed.

- **Ensure that resources, skills and preparation are sufficient to carry out the assignment or service**
  Assessors need to have access to ample resources to ensure that the assessment is sufficiently in-depth to reveal any areas of weakness within the candidate's profile. A good range of tests to assess for literacy and cognitive processing is needed so that the assessment criteria for each access arrangement can be covered. The assessor is then able to select appropriate tests, using the centre-based evidence to tailor the assessment to a candidate's individual needs.

  A well-trained assessor will have confidence in using tests and the necessary skills to make judgements about appropriate test resources, including those that are newly published.

  Preparation is an important factor in assessing for access arrangements, to ensure that procedures are followed correctly. The assessor must have information about

---

[13] The Patoss Code of Ethics is in the 'About Us' section of the website: https://www.patoss-dyslexia.org/About-Us/Code-of-Ethics

the learner's needs and normal way of working (i.e. Form 8 Part 1) before testing begins so that an assessment plan can be formulated that covers all the relevant areas to gain appropriate assessment evidence.

- **Update skills regularly both through relevant training and through learning activities**

  The JCQ regulations change each year. The changes can be minor but sometimes they are more extensive, and it is vital that assessors keep up-to-date. CPD courses can help assessors to ensure that their skills and knowledge remain current. It is also important to read the updated JCQ publications at the start of each academic year to ensure that any changes are understood.

  As new tests are added to an assessor's resources, it is important that the administration and scoring procedures are well understood and practised before they are used for a 'live' assessment. Publishers, test suppliers and training organisations sometimes have training videos or presentations on their websites which can be helpful, in addition to thorough scrutiny of the test manuals. Mentoring from, or observation of, a highly experienced assessor can also be a valuable training activity. Caution needs to be used when viewing test administration on online sites such as YouTube as the accuracy and quality cannot be verified.

- **Work collaboratively with relevant personnel including colleagues, advisers, parents and the client**

  Collaborative working is necessary within the whole access arrangements process and is a theme that runs through the JCQ regulations. Information is gathered from subject teachers and support staff and contributes to the centre-based evidence, which informs the assessment. The assessor feeds back and discusses the assessment results with the SENCo, who will draw everything together to make the decision about the access arrangements to be applied for.

  The candidate must be included within this process, and his views must be taken into account as it is pointless to put an access arrangement in place that the candidate does not want, does not find helpful and, ultimately, will not use.

Responsibility to the Client(s)

- **Consider the needs of the individual learner as paramount, subject to any legal constraints or ethical consideration**

  This is important for access arrangements assessments as a blanket approach will not meet the needs of all candidates. The assessment needs careful planning to take account of the background information and the JCQ assessment criteria so that relevant information is gained. However, the assessor needs to be flexible enough to adapt the assessment in light of information that arises during testing.

- **Respect the knowledge and experience, views, aims and preferences of the client**
  When planning an assessment session, it is important to remember that what works for one learner will not suit another. Consideration needs to be given to the testing environment, including whether group testing or a one-to-one arrangement will work better; the length of the assessment session and whether short breaks are needed between tests; and the type of test that is used to gather the required evidence.

- **Have the highest regard for the confidential nature of the work undertaken and individual records kept, safeguarding confidentiality at all times**
  The systems for storing and passing on information in relation to the access arrangements process within a centre need to be considered. Records must be stored securely by the SENCo (in line with GDPR requirements and school or college policy) for presentation to the JCQ Centre Inspector. The Examinations Officer will need to be informed of the approved access arrangements so that the arrangements can be put in place for examinations, including mock examinations and timed tests.

  Candidates who require access arrangements that need to be processed online must give their consent for this by signing the data protection notice. The signed notice is then stored within their file, and the files kept within a locked filing cabinet or in a secure electronic format.

  The assessor is responsible for storing assessment paperwork such as test forms. It is important that the integrity of the tests is maintained and that working papers (completed test forms) are not made available to non-specialists as this could compromise the test standardisation.[14] Relevant test results are recorded in the required format within JCQ Form 8 Part 2; test papers themselves are not required as evidence.

- **With the client's agreement, refer the client to another professional or another service where that is considered to be in the client's best interests, declaring any personal interest in such further work if it exists**
  This statement is concerned with assessors understanding the limitations of their skills, as previously discussed. Sometimes, a learner will require a more in-depth diagnostic assessment than can be provided through an access arrangements assessment. A preliminary interview with a learner may indicate that the case is complex, or the initial assessment may not get to the heart of the difficulties, so a fuller assessment is required. The learner will need to be referred to an alternative assessor if the access arrangements assessor is not qualified to conduct diagnostic assessments.

---

[14] SASC update issued August 2014, 'Assessors are also reminded that working papers from assessments should not be made available as these could affect the standardisation of the test.' Available at https://sasc.org.uk/SASC_Default.aspx?id=2 [Accessed 04.07.21].

In some cases, evidence of a hearing or vision difficulty may emerge in a pre-assessment interview or a mental health or medical problem may come to light. In each case, a referral will need to be made to the relevant professional so that the learner's needs can be addressed appropriately.

- **Ensure that, as appropriate, all programmes and advice are discussed and agreed with the client prior to being finalised**
  This reiterates the point about respecting learners' views and ensuring they have a voice and are involved in the process of determining access arrangements.

Professional independence and integrity

- **Avoid any action which might compromise their integrity and/or bring discredit on the profession**
  This speaks for itself. Assessors have a responsibility to conduct fair assessments, ensuring that tests are administered and scored in strict accordance with the instructions and to report the findings appropriately. To do otherwise could mean a learner gaining an unfair advantage over other candidates taking an examination or, conversely, could unfairly discriminate against a learner with a difficulty or disability.

- **Ensure that advice and recommendations are based on impartial consideration of all pertinent facts, circumstances and opinions derived from reliable and relevant sources**
  This is key to access arrangements assessments, as well as diagnostic assessments. The assessor must draw from an appropriately wide range of high-quality assessment resources to conduct accurate assessments, taking account of the background evidence and qualitative information gained during the assessment, thus ensuring that assessment evidence for access arrangements is based on valid and reliable results.

In summary...

Assessors must work with professional integrity. They must:
- Be suitably qualified to undertake the assessment work, and provide the centre with evidence of their qualifications;
- Use appropriate test resources and record the results in the correct format;
- Ensure that they update their skills and knowledge regularly;
- Work within their professional boundaries, referring a candidate to another professional when necessary.

Assessment purpose

There can be various reasons for carrying out an assessment for a learner in a secondary school or further education college.

Access arrangements

A 'standalone' access arrangements assessment is carried out purely for the purpose of gathering assessment evidence for the particular access arrangements (usually 25% extra time or a scribe) that a learner requires. This must be carried out no earlier than Year 9 and in accordance with the JCQ regulations.

Setting up a learning plan or programme of support

An assessment to build a picture of the learner's areas of strength and weakness, make recommendations for support and set up a support programme. This may involve carrying out one or more screening tests and some further literacy assessments.

Progress check

Following on from above, an assessment may be carried out at the end of an intervention or a support programme to measure a learner's progress and evaluate the success of the programme. For example, a learner may be involved in a 10-week spelling programme, with spelling tests being conducted at the start and the end.

Diagnostic assessment

In some settings, where resources allow, a diagnostic assessment may be undertaken if there are concerns over a student's progress in learning. The assessment report contains information about the learner's background and his performance in a range of standardised tests, together with recommendations for support. The assessment will include measures of underlying ability as well as literacy attainment and cognitive processing. Unlike JCQ Form 8, the report can provide a diagnosis of a specific learning difficulty such as dyslexia. This sort of a report, whilst extremely useful, cannot be used in place of Part 2 of JCQ Form 8.

Diagnostic assessments are also conducted by assessors working independently, whose services are engaged either by a parent, a learner or, in some cases, by a school or college that does not have a diagnostic assessor within the centre staff.

A diagnostic assessment that is carried out by a specialist assessor holding a current APC or an HCPC registered psychologist and that is conducted in accordance with SASC criteria can be used for support in higher education, including **Disabled Students Allowance (DSA).**[15] The diagnostic assessment report provides evidence of the learner's disability and means that further assessment is avoided.

---

[15] For more information on Disabled Students Allowance see https://www.gov.uk/disabled-students-allowances-dsas

Dual purpose assessments

Often, an assessment can be carried out for more than one purpose. For example, to investigate and identify a specific learning difficulty and also to gather assessment evidence for access arrangements. If the assessment is to be used for access arrangements, it is essential that:

- the assessor is suitably qualified to carry out the assessment and provides the centre with evidence of her qualification before the assessment takes place;
- the JCQ regulations are adhered to, including obtaining Part 1 from the centre prior to the assessment;
- the assessment evidence to support access arrangements is recorded within Form 8 Part 2.

This may mean that the assessment evidence is recorded in several ways, each one fulfilling a specific purpose, such as a diagnostic assessment report for support in university as well as Form 8 Part 2 for access arrangements in GCE A-level examinations.

In summary...

- There are various types of assessment that can be carried out within a school or college.
- If the assessment purpose includes gathering evidence for access arrangements, the assessor must be suitably qualified, must obtain JCQ Form 8 Part 1 before the assessment takes place and must record the results within JCQ Form 8 Part 2.

Selecting Appropriate Tests

The Assessment Plan

For access arrangements assessments, there is not a requirement to carry out a diagnostic assessment (in all but the rarest of cases - see page 119). The assessor must use appropriate assessment materials and assess the relevant areas to gain assessment evidence. The purpose of the assessment is to establish whether the results of tests in areas of literacy or cognitive processing provide evidence that the candidate has a difficulty that substantially affects learning and performance.

An access arrangements assessment will, very often, include fewer tests than would be used in a diagnostic assessment. The assessment materials that are used must be considered carefully to ensure that they are appropriate and provide robust evidence for access arrangements.

Having received a completed Form 8 Part 1, the assessor is able to proceed with the assessment. Part 1 provides a picture of the candidate's current areas of difficulty and any support that is in place for the candidate within the centre. An assessment plan can be formulated using this centre-based evidence as the basis for the assessment. This ensures that the assessment is tailored to the needs of each individual. For example, if teaching staff have reported that the candidate has difficulty working to time in the classroom, and extra time is used in tests and exams to enable the candidate to read text several times to absorb its meaning and to formulate written responses, the assessment plan will include measures relating to speed of working.

It is important that the plan is flexible as, whilst the assessor will have knowledge of the candidate's areas of need and normal way of working before the assessment, she cannot be sure of the performance during the assessment and outcomes. It may be necessary to include other assessments on the basis of what emerges during the assessment session itself.

Assessment is a specialised area and assessors should keep in mind the principle, *'Tests don't diagnose, people do.'* Whilst severe difficulties may be obvious, differentiating the genuine but less severe cases from the wide range of 'average' students can be complex. Standardised testing accompanied with careful questioning and observation are all part of a competent assessment and will reveal which aspects of literacy and processing are effortful and stress-inducing for the learner and can be especially helpful to the centre in making decisions about access arrangements. In addition, the student's approaches, strategies and responses in the test situation can feed into appropriate support, learning and revision strategies.

Assessment areas

The JCQ does not specify a prescribed list of tests that must be used for access arrangements assessments. Assessors must use their professional judgement and expertise to determine which tests to use in each case. There is no one assessment tool or package that covers all the areas that can provide assessment evidence for access arrangements. Assessors will need tests that cover the following:

Assessment area	Evidence for which access arrangement?
Spelling	Scribe
Writing speed	Scribe, Extra time
Reading speed of continuous text	Extra time
Cognitive processing (a range of measures covering different areas will be needed)	Extra time
Reading comprehension*	*Language modifier**
Vocabulary*	*Language modifier**

* A language modifier is a rare and exceptional access arrangement

In addition, assessors are likely to have access to a test of untimed word reading accuracy. Whilst assessment evidence is not required for a reader or computer reader, some centres find it helpful to have informal assessment information on a candidate's reading accuracy, comprehension and speed to inform their decision making around the allocation of reading support.

Once an assessor has built up a battery of tests it can be tempting to think that the job is done. However, this is not the case. Assessment resources continue to be developed and new editions made available. In addition, the access arrangements themselves and their assessment criteria can change from one year to the next.

It is important that assessors ensure that the tests they use remain current and continue to meet the requirements. Assessors should make sure that they check publishers and suppliers' websites regularly to maintain best practice regarding their assessment materials.

When a new test is added to the 'testing kit' the assessor will need to spend time reading through the test manual and studying the standardised test administration instructions and scoring procedures. Time will need to be spent practising using the test with willing volunteers before the test is used for an actual assessment. The necessity for time spent in careful preparation cannot be underestimated to ensure that results achieved are reliable.

JCQ guidance on test selection

Whilst specific tests are not stipulated, the JCQ AARA document does provide useful guidance on test choices within Chapter 7, 'Learning Difficulties'. We will consider this guidance in relation to test selection:

> The assessor must use current editions of nationally standardised tests appropriate to the candidate. [AARA 7.1.2]

This sentence provides general guidance about test materials, which is expanded upon later with two further statements, explored below. The idea that tests should be **appropriate to the candidate** supports the personalised, tailored nature of the access arrangements assessments; it is not a 'one size fits all' approach in which the same suite of tests is used for all candidates regardless of the nature of their particular difficulties and their normal way of working.

> Current editions of nationally standardised tests which produce standardised scores must be used, where published. [AARA 7.5.7]

This sentence contains plenty of guidance. Let's look at each part in turn:

Current editions

Tests that are in common use, that can be purchased through the publisher and for which test forms are available for purchase can be considered 'current editions.'

Ideally, tests that are used for an assessment will have been published within the last ten years for attainment tests or fifteen years for cognitive measures. Sometimes, however, this is not possible as there is no test published within that timeframe that covers the area being assessed.

When a new version of a test is published, it is considered best practice to use the most recent version of the test as soon as possible. Assessors should, ideally, switch to the latest version within two years of its publication date or sooner if they run out of examiner record forms. This ensures that the population that the test was standardised on (the norm group) is up-to-date and reflects the learner.

Nationally standardised tests

The norm group on which the test was standardised reflects the entire population of the country in which it was standardised; it is a nationally representative sample of the general population. The sample group is taken from the whole country rather than a localised area within it. This means that scores achieved in a testing session can be compared against the scores of typical students of the same age across the population of the country.

Ideally, particularly for attainment tests, assessors will select tests that have been normed on a UK population, so that the norm group reflects the UK education system. This is not always possible, however, as tests using UK norms are not available for all areas that provide assessment evidence for access arrangements.

Standardised scores

The assessment evidence for access arrangements must be reported as standard scores with a mean of 100. Other types of standardised score, such as z-scores and t-scores cannot be used. Percentiles and age-equivalent scores cannot be used. Some tests provide subtest scores as scaled scores (with a mean of 10). These must be converted to standard scores for use on Form 8 Part 2. This can be done easily using a conversion chart (see page 111).

Where published

It is not sufficient to use assessment materials that fall outside these criteria if there are published tests that meet these requirements. As assessors, we should seek to use the best tools that are available, so that we can be confident in the results they produce. Whilst the 'ideal' test materials do not always exist, it could be argued that there are published materials that fulfil these criteria for each area of testing that provides assessment evidence for access arrangements.

> The candidate's chronological age must be less than the 'ceiling' of the test unless no test is published for the candidate's age. [AARA 7.5.8]

In this context, the 'ceiling' or 'ceiling age' of the test is the highest age that the test has been standardised for; the top age within the norm group. Ideally, assessors will select tests for which the candidate's age is well within the age norms, as those closest to the extremes can be slightly less reliable statistically.

For school-aged learners, tests are available for all areas providing assessment evidence. For older learners aged 25 or older in further education there are a few assessment areas for which there is no test published for the learner's age group. At the time of publication, there is no test of free writing speed available for learners aged over 25 and the tests assessing phonological processing for this age group are restricted to assessors with certain qualifications. In this situation, it is permissible to use tests with a ceiling age lower than the candidate's age if all other avenues have been explored.

Where no test is published for an older learner in an area that could provide assessment evidence, the best way to proceed is as follows:

- Explore other areas that provide assessment evidence for the particular access arrangements being sought.

  For example, for a candidate who requires a scribe, tests of free writing speed and spelling can provide assessment evidence. The starting point would be to assess spelling as tests with high ceiling ages are available.

  For a candidate who requires extra time, tests of text reading speed, writing speed and cognitive processing can provide assessment evidence. Begin with measures of text reading speed and areas of cognitive processing (such as working memory) as tests with high ceiling ages are available.

- If testing in the other areas provides the required assessment evidence, this can be reported within Form 8 Part 2 and no further assessment is required.

- If testing in the other areas does not give the required scores, proceed to assessing the candidate using the test with the ceiling age lower than his chronological age.

- Calculate the standard score for the ceiling age of the test.

- If this standard score based on the ceiling age norms meets the assessment evidence requirements, record the score within Form 8 Part 2.

- Add a note within the 'Other Relevant Information' area of Part 2 to explain that the score for the ceiling age has been reported and the test has been used as there is no test published for the candidate's age group which assesses this area.

Please note: This procedure is not used for full diagnostic assessments of older learners.

Other considerations when selecting standardised tests

Valid and Reliable

Assessors need to ensure that the assessment tools provide valid and reliable results; in other words, that they measure what they claim to, and that they produce consistent results. (See Chapter 8 for further discussion of psychometrics.)

Cost-effective

School and college budgets, as you will be all too well aware, are not limitless. For this reason, it is important that the test resources represent good value for money whilst, at the same time, meeting JCQ requirements and producing robust results. Points to consider are:

- How much the test costs initially.
  The initial outlay is an important factor, but it is not the only consideration.

- Whether the full test kit needs to be purchased or if parts are sold individually.
  For some tests, only certain sections are needed which can be bought separately.

- What the ongoing costs are.
  Do you need to purchase test forms or does the test permit photocopying of materials? Do you need to purchase online scoring credits or an annual licence?

- Whether the test covers more than one area of testing.
  Some test batteries include a range of subtests covering various areas of literacy attainment and cognitive processing, some or all of which can provide assessment evidence. These tests are often expensive. Other tests cover only one of the assessment criteria (e.g. spelling) but may be much cheaper to buy and use.

Time-effective

- Consider how quick and easy the test is to administer and score.

- Can it be administered to a group or must it be used individually? Note: Any group assessments must always be administered by a suitably qualified assessor.

Group tests and Individual tests

Assessment evidence for Form 8 Part 2 can come from assessments that have been administered either in a group or individually. Whilst some areas of testing can be administered to a small group, such as writing speed and spelling accuracy, individual assessment will be needed for any tests that require a verbal response or that require individual timing. Just as for individual assessment, for information from group testing to be included within Form 8 Part 2, the testing must be conducted by a suitably qualified assessor, it cannot be delegated to another member of staff.

Below are some possible advantages and disadvantages of group and individual assessment.

Advantages of group assessment	Disadvantages of group assessment
• Time efficient • Cost-effective • Learner may feel more at ease in a group	• Difficult to observe individual responses • Tests may not suit all learners • Not possible in all areas • Learner may feel ill at ease in a group • Harder to manage
Advantages of individual assessment	**Disadvantages of individual assessment**
• Learner responses easier to observe • Tailored to the individual • One session can cover all areas • Easier to manage	• More time needed • Less cost effective

Paper-based and Computer-based assessments

The traditional method of assessment has been to use paper-based assessments, administering and scoring the assessment by hand. As technology advances, there has been an increase in assessment tools that are either administered or scored, or both, by computer. For example:

- A test kit supplied with an accompanying a memory stick containing the manual and scoring pages.

- A test that is administered by hand and then scored using a computer. The raw scores are entered and the computer program provides the standard scores.

- A test that is administered and scored using the computer. Such tests can be administered in a face-to-face setting or, where necessary remotely. (See pages 100 to 102 for more information on remote assessment.)

Such tests need to be evaluated using the same stringent criteria as paper-based assessments to ensure that they provide valid and reliable results. Each part of the test battery needs to be considered in relation to the JCQ criteria to ensure that it meets the evidence requirements.

Whilst computer-based tests can sometimes be seen as a 'quick and easy' way to gather assessment evidence, it is important to remember that, just as for paper-based assessments, no single test can provide assessment evidence across all the JCQ criteria. Assessors will need to have a variety of tests, which may be paper-based or computer-based, to select from to ensure that the assessment is tailored and meets the individual needs of all candidates.

As with paper-based assessments, the person who is administering the test must be suitably qualified to assess for access arrangements. Whilst it may seem that some computer-based assessment tools do not require much administration from an assessor, this is simply not correct. The assessor must be vigilant in observing the assessment behaviour of learners who are taking the test and follow up with individual discussions to review aspects of the testing performance and approaches to tasks. Information can also be gathered about other areas of assessment that may be required as a follow-up to the computer-based assessment. For example, an assessor's observations of a learner taking a computer-based reading assessment and the follow-up discussion with the learner may provide indications of a processing difficulty that can be explored through further assessment of processing using either a paper-based test or another computer-based tool.

If a computer-based assessment is carried out by someone who does not hold an appropriate qualification in assessment, the results cannot be used as assessment evidence in Form 8 Part 2, they are only able to be used as screening test results within Part 1. Some centres opt to use computer-based assessment as a starting point, recording the results in Part 1, before following up with paper-based assessment with the results recorded in Part 2. Other centres select from computer-based and paper-based assessment materials for the assessment results that are used within Part 2. Provided that the assessment tools and the test results meet the JCQ criteria and any testing for Part 2 is conducted by a qualified assessor, either approach is acceptable.

Screening tests
Only fully standardised diagnostic assessment tools are able to be used to provide assessment evidence for Form 8 Part 2. The results of screening tests cannot be used for this purpose. Screening tests are useful in a number of ways, but they are not suitable for providing core assessment evidence for access arrangements.

Many centres use screening tests results as part of the centre-based evidence within Form 8 Part 1. This can be a useful approach in providing a snapshot of a learner's areas of strength and difficulty, which can be followed up by a more in-depth assessment using appropriate tests for Form 8 Part 2.

Remote assessment

The usual method of carrying out an assessment is with the assessor and the candidate in a face-to-face setting. Wherever possible this should continue to be how assessment sessions are conducted. However, in 2020-2021, during periods of lockdown in the Covid-19 pandemic, it became necessary to consider alternative methods of assessment for candidates requiring assessment information in Form 8 Part 2 to evidence their need for access arrangements.

For the past 10 to 15 years, it has been possible to use the internet for remote assessment in some areas. Such assessments have been necessary in very particular circumstances, for example, for candidates in the Falkland Islands taking UK qualifications where there is no qualified assessor to conduct an in-person assessment.

In recent years, publishers have moved towards providing digital versions of assessment materials alongside print versions and this has facilitated computer-based assessment.

As Covid-19 pandemic restrictions began to affect the possibility of face-to-face contact, assessors began to consider the feasibility of conducting assessments remotely using a video link. A greater range of digital resources were made available and publishers produced detailed guidance to explain exactly how and in what types of situations these copyrighted materials could be used with 'teleconferencing' remote software. In addition, at various points during 2020-2021, the SpLD Assessment Standards Committee (SASC) produced guidance on conducting assessments remotely[16].

It is worth noting that most of the assessment resources used in both diagnostic assessments for SpLD and in access arrangements assessments have been standardised for in-person testing and most test publishers consider remote administration of tests (i.e. using a video link, with the assessor and the candidate in different locations) to be an adaptation. Whilst the tests used for access arrangements assessments have not yet been restandardised to establish new norms for remote use, some publishers are researching the correlation between assessment data obtained from in-person assessments and remote assessments. Whilst this is still in the early stages, there is evidence to support a level of equivalence for some types of tests when administered face-to-face and remotely[17].

In 2020, the JCQ issued the following advice regarding remote assessments[18]:

> 'Access Arrangements Assessors may need to consider carrying out assessments with social distancing measures in place or, as a last resort, remotely via an online video call.

---

[16] SASC Guidance on Remote Diagnostic Assessments March 2021 - updated 10 May 2021, www.sasc.org.uk/downloads [Accessed July 2021]

[17] Pearson: Telepractice norms and validity of performance-based tests. Available from: https://www.pearsonclinical.co.uk/Sitedownloads/telepractice/telepractice-norms-and-validity-of-performance-based-tests.pdf [Accessed July 2021]

[18] JCQ (2020) Important supplementary information for SENCos and Assessors, Academic Year 2020-21, available at https://qualifications.pearson.com/content/dam/pdf/Support/Access-arrangements/Supplementary-AA-guidance-202021.pdf [Accessed July 2021]

Ideally, assessments will be carried out in the physical presence of the candidate. Many test publishers have provided resources and guidance to facilitate remote assessment. Where assessment can be delayed (rather than be conducted remotely) assessors should wait until it is possible to meet with the candidate.

SASC has issued guidance on remote assessment and assessment with social distancing measures in place. Test scores recorded within Part 2 of Form 8 must be obtained from an assessment that has been conducted in accordance with professional advice and within publishers' guidelines.'

Where an assessment has been conducted remotely, the assessor should note within the 'Other Relevant Information' section of Form 8 Part 2 that the assessment was conducted in a remote setting using video conferencing facilities.

At the time of writing, restrictions are being eased and face-to-face assessments are now possible. However, we cannot yet know the extent to which remote assessment will continue to be a necessary option. The JCQ guidance remains that remote assessment may need to be considered in exceptional circumstances, and it is vital that assessors develop robust assessment protocols.

Conducting an assessment remotely presents a unique set of challenges that need to be considered and overcome. Assessors will need to ensure that they keep up-to-date with current SASC guidance[19] and work within publishers' requirements. Ideally, assessors will undertake training or mentoring on remote assessment before carrying out such work.

Evaluating a test

As the JCQ does not provide a list of tests that are acceptable for access arrangements assessments, assessors will need to evaluate tests that are available to determine whether they will be appropriate and useful for assessments with their setting.

The following page contains a set of questions that tests can be checked against, to consider whether they meet the needs of learners in your setting. However, keep in mind that tests are rarely perfect, so you must balance their strengths and weaknesses to make a judgement.

Lists of tests available for use in access arrangements assessments

Chapter 10 contains lists of tests that are useful for access arrangements assessments. The tables include information on the tests, their ceiling ages and which areas of assessment

---

[19] Current guidance regarding remote assessment and test materials can be found on the SASC website: https://sasc.org.uk/

evidence they can be used for. It is important to remember that the list is current at the time of publication. Annual updates to the list will be provided on the Patoss website.

Is the test "a good fit" with my students?	
• When was it published? Do I have the most up-to-date edition?	It is important to compare candidates against the most up-to-date information available, to give a fair representation of the population now. It is recommended that tests are no more than 10 years old for attainment tests and no more than 15 years old for cognitive processing tests. It is recommended to switch to the most recent edition within 2 years of publication.
• What age range does it cover?	The test should more than span the age of the candidate, as results at the very edges of test ranges are less reliable.
• Has it been standardised using a large and diverse sample population?	A better and bigger sample will more likely include similar individuals to the candidate and thus give a fairer comparison (see Chapter 8).
• Where was it developed?	A UK test will be preferable if one is available, although English language USA tests are fully acceptable.
• Will the format of the test work for my students?	A good test needs to be accessible in terms of print, layout, paper quality and the provision of practice items. If computer-based, could layouts or IT requirements influence the results?
Is the test "a good fit" with the assessment needs?	
• Does the test consistently measure what it claims to measure? Is it valid and reliable?	A valid and reliable test ensures the test activities are good tools to measure target skills and that results are consistent. (See Chapter 8 for discussion of test validity and reliability.)
• Does the manual give standard scores?	Standard scores based on a mean of 100 are required within Form 8 Part 2 and by AAO. Scaled scores (with a mean of 10) can be converted.
• Is it an individual and/or group test?	Group tests can help with the workload but do not allow close investigation of individual strengths and weaknesses.
• Does the test measure a range of skills or areas?	A test battery that provides assessment evidence across a range of areas can be a versatile tool in addressing individual needs.
• Will this test fit into my work environment? What are the ongoing costs?	The best test in the world is no good if it takes so long to administer, mark and score you could never fit it into your working day!

8. Basic Concepts in Psychometrics

This chapter provides a brief overview of the most important issues an assessor must understand when choosing, using, scoring and interpreting the results of standardised tests in an educational setting. It should be noted that some of the information will not be used directly when conducting an access arrangements assessment, but it is important information for all assessors using standardised tests.

Quantitative and Qualitative Data

Quantitative data involves information that can be measured. It is the objective measurement or scoring of performance and allows for statistical analysis and comparison.

There are a variety of ways in which we can compare performance. As teachers, we seek to measure the progress of individuals by comparing their performance in a particular task or skill over time. For example, we may wish to evaluate the success of a spelling intervention and so we will measure their spelling ability at the start of the support and again at the end, to see if performance has improved.

Within diagnostic assessment, an assessor will conduct testing in a range of areas and compare performance in one domain against another. For example, an assessor will consider a learner's reading comprehension in relation to his verbal ability.

A third way that quantitative data allows for comparison is when an individual's performance is assessed against others within the same age group. This is the basis for standardised assessment and is a vital part of the access arrangements process. An individual's score is converted to a scale based on their age group to determine whether performance is at the expected level for his age, better than average or below average compared to others of the same age within the standardisation sample (the norm group). We will look at the use of standardised scores in more detail later.

Qualitative data is, as the name suggests, a more subjective measure of an individual's performance. However, it is a vital part of both diagnostic assessment and access arrangements assessment. The gathering of qualitative information seeks to explain and understand performance. Observation of a learner's performance behaviour helps the assessor to understand and explain how and why the learner has achieved a particular score, whether it is high or low. The assessor considers the strategies that a learner has used in a particular assessment task; and whether they were effective, leading to a high score. If a low score is achieved, qualitative observation can help to explain the reasons; for example, the learner may have adopted poor strategies, become distracted and lost focus or misread a question.

The gathering of both quantitative and qualitative data is integral to the access arrangements process, helping to determine and provide the necessary evidence for appropriate access arrangements.

The centre-based evidence will include a wealth of qualitative data, such as observations from teaching and support staff regarding a learner's classroom behaviour; evidence of the support and access arrangements that are in place for internal tests and mock examinations; and a student's self-reported difficulties. The evidence from a centre may also include some quantitative data, such as the results of screening tests and previous diagnostic assessments and evidence of higher scores when extra time is provided in tests.

Within the access arrangements assessment, the quantitative data is the scores achieved on the standardised tests, as recorded within Form 8 Part 2. However, it is important to remember that qualitative information has a vital part to play in the assessment process. The assessor's observations and sensitive questioning of the learner can help to inform appropriate access arrangements. For example, a learner may opt to read out loud in a reading comprehension task when given the choice to do so, as it helps with processing the written information. This reading behaviour may not have been evident within a classroom setting and could help to show that the option to read aloud in examinations would be an appropriate arrangement.

Choosing standardised tests

Every time we look up an individual's test results in norms tables, we are in effect comparing his performance with that of the group used during the test development and standardisation, the norm group. The larger the group and more widely distributed across different areas (inner city, suburban, rural, etc.) the more likely it is that the statistics regarding what is average, above average and below, are meaningful and 'true' for the population as a whole.

Furthermore, since language, literacy standards and other attributes within both school and general populations are constantly evolving, norms established several decades ago may not be fair representations of the population now.

Reliability

The reliability of a test reflects the extent to which it produces stable and consistent results. There are many ways of assessing reliability, each with its own advantages and so reliability is not a fixed quantity. You will find details of the methods used in each test in its manual.

An often-quoted measure of internal reliability is known as Cronbach's Alpha. This checks to see what proportion of the candidates get questions of differing difficulty correct. For example, only the best should get the hardest ones correct. Values of 0.8 or higher indicate well-designed and balanced tests that should enable differentiation to occur.

Other important aspects of test reliability are:

Test-retest reliability: This is obtained by administering the same test twice over a set period of time to the same group. The scores are correlated to evaluate the test for stability over time. Should testing need to be repeated, assessors should check the manual to see how soon the same test can be administered again.

Inter-scorer reliability: This is used to assess the degree to which the assessment decisions of different scorers agree. This is useful because human observers will not necessarily interpret answers the same way.

Parallel forms reliability: This is obtained by administering different versions of an assessment tool to the same group of individuals. The scores from the two versions can then be correlated in order to evaluate the consistency of results across alternate versions.

> **Action:** Look for reliability values of at least 0.8 and preferably above 0.9. The higher the reliability, the greater confidence you can have concerning the candidate's real ability based on that particular test result.

Validity

Validity studies tell you to what extent the test measures what it says it does. It is vital for a test to be valid in order for the results to be accurately applied and interpreted. Again, there are different ways of measuring validity because there are different aspects. Some main ones are:

Content validity: This relates to how well the test covers all the relevant aspects of the skills being assessed. This can involve consideration of the rationale and research base for selecting items.

Construct validity: This is used to ensure that the test measures what it is intended to measure, the construct, and not other variables. This can involve analysis of the test items by a panel of experts familiar with the construct.

Criterion-related validity: This considers the relationship between performances on this test and another criterion of interest. *Concurrent validity* measures the how well the scores on the test correlate with a well-established test. *Predictive validity* seeks to establish whether results can predict future performance. For example, learners with decoding difficulties would be expected to have low scores on a new nonword decoding test.
Much information regarding validity is expressed in terms of correlations with other variables. Correlation coefficients express the relationship between two variables but do not necessarily mean that one causes the other, although it may. For example, there is a very

high correlation between children's reading ability and the size of their feet – because they both increase with age (the underlying factor), but neither causes the other!

> **Action:** Choose a test which focuses on and measures the precise skills you wish to investigate. Select tests that provide sound evidence of their validity for the purpose.

Using standardised tests

A principal characteristic of standardised tests is that administration procedures, stimulus materials and scoring are prescribed, are exactly the same for all who use and take them and match precisely the method used when the test was standardised. Since all candidates have (as near as possible) the same test experience, differences in scores should, therefore, reflect true differences in ability.

Validity and reliability also involve the assessor in selecting an appropriate test and using it properly. As assessors, our actions can impact on the accuracy of the results we gain from assessment. We must choose appropriate tests, taking account of the learner and the information we wish to gain, and administer and score the tests correctly to ensure that the results are reliable. When a standardised test is used, the same testing experience must be recreated for every learner every time, no matter who is testing them. In this way the performance of the learner who has been assessed can be compared with learners of the same age in the norm group.

> **Action:** Make sure you know and follow the precise procedures for administration of any test that you use. The manual will usually tell you the exact words to use and whether (for example) you may repeat or rephrase a question.

Understanding test scores

Normal Distribution
It is essential for assessors to have a good understanding of normal distribution as it is the basis of the scoring in both diagnostic assessment and access arrangements assessment. Most tests of ability and attainment, if administered to a large, representative sample of the population, produce roughly bell-shaped (normal) distributions with lots of people scoring in the middle, or average, range (the 'central tendency') and far fewer having extreme (very high or very low) results.

The familiar 'bell-shaped curve' is the graphical representation of normal distribution. The central point of the distribution is the mean, shown in the diagram below as the central line. Most data values occur near the mean, producing a single peak in the middle. In standardised tests, the mean is the arithmetic average score for the standardisation sample group. The curve is symmetrical with half of the data values occurring above the mean and half below the mean. The curve tapers at each end, with fewer scores occurring the further away from the mean in either direction.

To find how the scores are distributed around the mean, we measure the variation in the scatter of scores by calculating the standard deviation (SD). The SD is the 'average' amount by which scores differ from the mean, regardless of direction.

The bell curve is sliced into vertical parts which are each one standard deviation wide. The curve represents the whole set of test scores (100%) and fixed proportions of test scores lie within each of the sections, or standard deviations, of the curve.

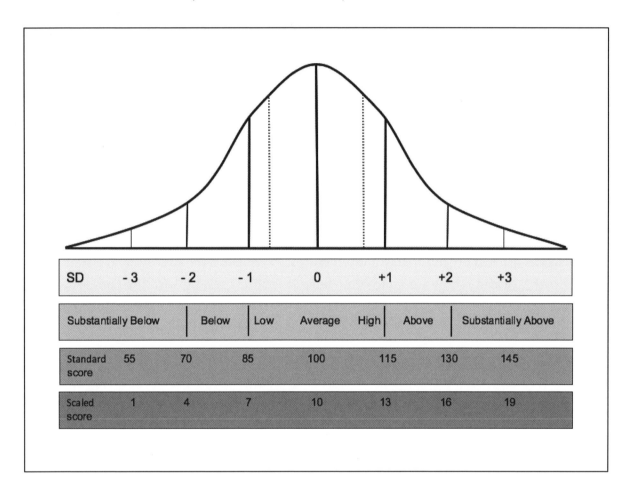

SD	- 3	- 2	- 1	0	+1	+2	+3
	Substantially Below		Below	Low	Average	High	Above	Substantially Above
Standard score	55	70	85	100	115	130	145
Scaled score	1	4	7	10	13	16	19

Normal Distribution Curve

Roughly two-thirds, 68%, of the population fall within one standard deviation either side of the mean, and this is the 'average range.' Approximately 95% of the score sample will fall within two standard deviations of the mean and around 99% of the score sample will be within three standard deviations of the mean. Scores more than three standard deviations beyond the mean are very rare.

To help with the interpretation and comparison of scores, test developers use a 'standardised normal distribution' to produce different types of standardised scores, including the standard scores that are used in access arrangements assessments.

Raw scores

The raw score in a test might simply be the number of correct items, for example, 6 words out of 10 spelt correctly in a spelling test could give a raw score of 6. Sometimes other scoring systems are used, for example, one point being awarded for each digit recalled correctly in a sequence. In tests which have entry points for different age groups, items before the entry point are usually counted in the raw score.

As each test has its own scale, raw scores cannot be directly compared with the scores in other tests. For this reason, raw scores are converted to derived scores, so that performance can be compared to the reference group for the test. Using a common scale also means that the scores from different tests can be compared with each other.

Standardised scores: standard scores and scaled scores.

Test developers produce tables of 'norms' which tell us about the expected performance of specific groups, usually based on age. Standardised scores show the candidate's position relative to the mean for his age group; the mean is the calculated average for the age group in the standardisation sample.

Standard scores have a mean of 100 and a standard deviation of 15. These are the scores that are used for access arrangements assessments and reported within Form 8 Part 2.

Scaled scores are less precise than standard scores; they have a mean of 10 and a standard deviation of 3. Scaled scores are quite often used for subtest scores, with the composite given as a standard score. Scaled scores can be converted to standard scores by using a conversion chart like the one on the next page. Alternatively, use the formula:

$$\textbf{scaled score x 5 + 50 = standard score}$$

Percentile scores reflect the percentage of the group whose scores fall below that of the candidate. Imagine a line-up of 100 individuals of the same age of our learner; where the learner is placed in that line-up of 100 is their percentile rank. If they are 50th in the line, they are exactly average. A score at the 10th percentile is low (90% of the test standardisation sample for their age group performed better) as the learner is 10th from the bottom in the line-up. A 90th percentile rank is high as only 10% of the test standardisation sample for their age group exceeded this score.

Because of normal distribution, there is relatively little difference between the raw scores of a large percentage of individuals whose results are near the mean. Thus, percentiles between 16 and 84 are 'within the average range'. Percentile scores, therefore, can magnify small differences near the mean which may not be significant; and reduce the apparent size of large differences near the tails of the curve, i.e. the difference, in terms of actual performance, between percentile ranks 5 and 15 is far larger than that between percentile ranks 40 and 50. Standardised scores avoid this since the intervals are all equal. Percentiles are not used in access arrangements and are not reported in Form 8 Part 2.

Converting Scaled Scores with a mean of 10
to
Standard Scores with a mean of 100

Scaled Score	Standard Score
1	55
2	60
3	65
4	70
5	75
6	80
7	85
8	90
9	95
10	100
11	105
12	110
13	115
14	120
15	125
16	130
17	135
18	140
19	145

Age Equivalent scores

A third type of derived score is the age equivalent. It tells you the chronological age, or age range, for which a particular raw score is average. However, reporting age equivalents can be a sensitive and emotive area (imagine reporting that a 15-year-old learner has the reading age of a 7-year-old). In addition, age equivalents become less and less appropriate as the age of the candidate increases, since the rate of development of skills and attainment decreases. For these reasons, age equivalent scores are not used in either diagnostic assessment or access arrangements.

Level descriptors and score ranges

Different test publishers use a variety of verbal labels to describe different sections of the normal curve, which can be confusing. In addition, tests published in the USA and the UK tend to use different scores to describe the average range. For clarity, many assessors stick to the statistical divisions based on standard deviations, and this reflects the JCQ approach. This would lead to the following:

Standard score	Level descriptor
Below 70	Substantially below average
70 - 84	Below average
85 - 89	Low average
90 - 110	Mid average
111 - 115	High average
116 - 130	Above average
Above 130	Substantially above average

Subtests and composites

Many tests offer the opportunity to bring together the scores on a number of subtests to provide a combined measure of a skill; the subtests measure one particular skill within a domain whilst the composite (sometimes known as the Index) represents the overall score for the domain, bringing together related skills. Generally, the composite score is more statistically reliable than the subtest scores. Both subtest and composite scores can be used in assessments for access arrangements and reported within Form 8 Part 2.

Confidence Intervals and Standard Error of Measurement

Confidence intervals (or confidence bands or confidence ranges) provide a range of test scores within which we can be confident that the "true" measure of the candidate's skill lies. These ranges are calculated using the standard error of measurement (SEM); they are a statistical measurement and nothing to do with the candidate being ill or 'having a bad day'.

There is always the possibility of a discrepancy between a person's 'true' score and obtained score because of the imperfect reliability of any test. The SEM is the likely size of this discrepancy and the confidence intervals are based on SEMs. There is an inverse relationship between the reliability coefficient of a test and its SEM. A highly reliable test will have a small SEM and so each obtained score is likely to be close to the hypothetically 'true' one.

Most test manuals provide data regarding standard errors of measurement (SEM) and confidence intervals – either on the examiner record form, in norms tables, on the online scoring platform, or in their chapter on test reliability. Some manuals publish tables giving the confidence interval directly but if they do not it can be calculated from the SEM data. Confidence intervals are usually defined thus:

- It is 68% certain that a person's true score will be within the band of scores lying 1 SEM either side of his obtained score. This is the 68% confidence interval.
- It is 95% certain that it will be within plus/minus 2 SEMs of his obtained score.
- It is 99% certain for the range 3 SEMs either side of the obtained score.

In SpLD diagnostic assessment reports, the 95% confidence interval is used.

When calculating the 95% CI for standard scores, multiply the SEM by 2 and then add to/subtract from the standard score. The chart below shows summarises this process:

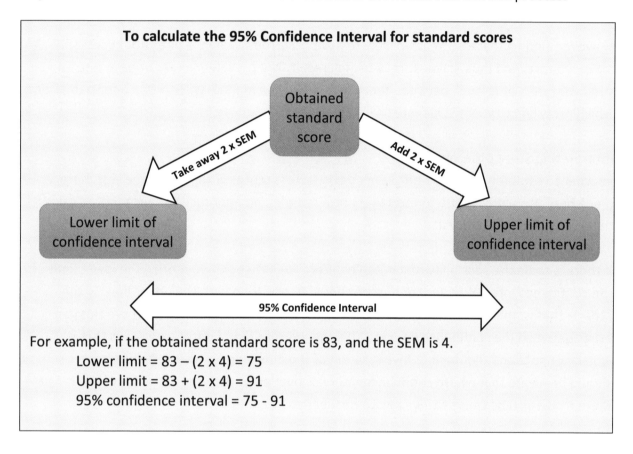

To calculate the 95% Confidence Interval for standard scores

For example, if the obtained standard score is 83, and the SEM is 4.
Lower limit = 83 − (2 x 4) = 75
Upper limit = 83 + (2 x 4) = 91
95% confidence interval = 75 - 91

When calculating the 95% CI for scaled scores, there is an extra step to follow. You will report the scores as standard scores so, firstly, convert the scaled score to a standard score. Next multiply the SEM by 2 *and then by 5 (this is the extra step)*. Subtract this figure from the standard score for the lower CI limit; add it to the standard score for the upper CI limit.

For example, if the obtained scaled score is 5, and the SEM (for the scaled score) is 1:

Step 1 – Convert scaled score to standard score: 5 is converted to 75.
Step 2 – Multiply the SEM by 2 **and then by 5**: 1 x 2 = 2, **and then 2 x 5 = 10**
Step 3 - Subtract from/add to the standard score: 75 – 10 = 65; 75 + 10 = 85

Therefore, the standard score is 75 and its 95% confidence interval is 65 – 85.

Note: Whilst it is important to know about them, confidence intervals are not used in access arrangements assessments. They are not quoted in Form 8 Part 2.

Statistical significance, Probability and Prevalence

Test manuals provide information about the significance of the results given as Probability coefficients (p). These tell you about the likelihood of getting a particular result, or set of results, by chance. The smaller the p is (e.g. 0.05, 0.01, 0.001) the more significant the result; i.e. it would have been very unlikely to have occurred by chance.

However, finding that a score is unlikely to have occurred by chance does not necessarily make it a rare, and thus diagnostically useful, result. The prevalence rate or base rate tells you how rare a difference between the scores is and the manual will contain information on which prevalence rates are diagnostically interesting.

Interpreting Score Differences

In order to establish if notable differences exist across scores within the same test battery (i.e. where the scores relate to the same norm sample), an approach can be adopted using the 95% confidence interval.

If there is to be the possibility of a notable difference between two scores, the lower limit of the confidence interval around one score should not overlap with the upper limit of the other – that is, the confidence intervals should be clear of one another.[20] Where this gap exists between the confidence intervals this can indicate that a difference exists that is worthy of note and that further investigation of the difference is warranted. Assessors should be aware that where confidence intervals overlap at the very extremes of the range there might also be cause to investigate further.

---

[20] Johnson, B. et al (2011, updated 2020) *The Standard Error of Measurement and Confidence Intervals.* Available at: https://www.patoss-dyslexia.org/write/MediaUploads/Resources/Standard_Error_of_Measurement_and_Confidence_Intervals_PATOSS_Updated_June_2020.pdf

9. Assessment Criteria for Access Arrangements

In this chapter, we will discuss the assessment evidence for the main access arrangements that need to be applied for through Access Arrangements Online.

Please remember, centre-based evidence is always required alongside the assessment evidence and this is discussed in Chapter 6.

25% extra time

For 25% extra time, Form 8 with assessment evidence is needed for candidates with cognition and learning needs who do not have an EHCP, IDP or SEN Statement.

The most common access arrangement requiring online approval is 25% extra time. It can require some of the most detailed investigation and clarity of evidence to arrive at a fair conclusion. More than one score is needed and a variety of literacy and processing tests that can provide evidence for extra time will be used. The difficulties that have been reported within Form 8 Part 1 will help the assessor to determine which areas of assessment and, in turn, which tests to focus on. Unsurprisingly, the areas that can provide assessment are connected with speed of working. The standard assessment evidence is, as a minimum:

- Two below average standard scores of 84 or less
- One below average standard score of 84 or less and one low average standard score of 85 – 89

The standard scores must relate to two (or more) different areas of speed of working, as follows:

- Speed of reading and speed of writing
- Speed of reading and cognitive processing
- Speed of writing and cognitive processing
- Two different areas of cognitive processing which impact on speed of working[21]

Speed of reading
Where a candidate reads independently (i.e. they do not use a reader or computer reader), a reading speed score that is recorded in Form 8 Part 2 may be used as one of the two required measures for 25% extra time. It must relate to the speed of reading continuous text, not single word reading.

---

[21] JCQ (2020) Access Arrangements and Reasonable Adjustments, 5.2.2, available at www.jcq.org.uk

There are various measures of text reading speed that are acceptable to use:

- A timed reading comprehension providing one score for comprehension, based on the number of items answered correctly, and a separate score for speed, based on the time taken to read the entire text or the amount of text read within an allotted time. The speed score (also called reading rate) can provide evidence for extra time. The comprehension score cannot be used as evidence for extra time.

- A combined measure of text reading accuracy and speed. This is usually known as reading fluency. The score is based on the number of words read correctly within a given time, or the number of words correctly and the time taken to read the entire text.

- A test that provides a score for the time taken to both read text and answer comprehension questions. This is usually known as reading comprehension speed (but can also be known as reading fluency or reading speed). It is not the same as a timed reading comprehension. The latter provides a score only for measuring the understanding of the text rather than **time** taken to process and understand what has been read.

Another type of timed reading test is one that measures word reading under closely timed conditions. This provides a score for word reading efficiency. It may also include a closely timed measure of nonsense word reading, to assess how efficiently phonic decoding skills can be employed. The score is based on how many words or non-words are read in the allotted time. Tests of **reading efficiency** are able to be used as assessment evidence for extra time – however, the score is recorded on Form 8 as a measure of cognitive processing (See next page).

Speed of writing

Where a candidate writes independently (i.e. they do not use a scribe, speech recognition technology, or a word processor), a writing speed score that is recorded in the 25% extra time section of Form 8 Part 2 may be used as one of the two required measures for 25% extra time. The score must relate to an assessment of handwriting speed (i.e. the candidate writes by hand, not using a word processor).

Commonly, a measure of free writing speed is used. In a test of free writing, the candidate is provided with a topic to write about and must generate ideas and put his thoughts down in writing, under timed conditions. The number of words produced provides a words-per-minute (wpm) score which is converted to a standard score for use as assessment evidence. (Note: a wpm score cannot be used as assessment evidence, it must be converted to a standard score for recording within Form 8 Part 2.)

Other measures of writing speed can also provide assessment evidence for extra time. These include:

- a test of writing fluency, which requires the candidate to formulate and write sentences or short pieces of text under timed conditions. The stimuli for the writing might be pictures to respond to, key words to include in the written response, or short phrases used as sentence starters;

- a standardised dictation at text level for which the candidate must write by hand. The dictation is delivered in stages and the candidate is required to write, under timed conditions, what has been said;

- a composite score for writing speed which is made up of a variety of handwriting speed tasks. Each task is completed under timed conditions to give an overall score for handwriting speed.

Cognitive processing measures which have a substantial and long-term adverse effect on speed of working

As noted above, a minimum of two scores relating to different areas of speed of working must be recorded within Form 8 Part 2 as assessment evidence for 25% extra time. The two scores can relate to different areas of cognitive processing.

In days gone by, it may have been acceptable to carry out just one or two assessments relating to speed of working to gain the required evidence for 25% extra time. Some assessors may have focused almost entirely on literacy assessments of reading and writing speeds. However, the criteria have changed and this approach is no longer sufficient. A more detailed investigation of cognitive processing is now required and, for this reason, an assessor will need to have a range of cognitive processing measures available to ensure that different areas of processing are considered.

There are a variety of tests available measuring different areas of cognitive processing. The AARA document sets out examples of assessment areas to consider.[22] These include measures of phonological skills, short term and working memory, visual and visual-motor processing, and other tests measuring the fluency and efficiency of performing cognitive tasks. A test of mathematical processing can be used in certain circumstances and is discussed in detail on the next page.

When selecting tests to provide assessment evidence for extra time, consideration needs to be given to the impact on speed of working. For example:

- A test of rapid naming can evidence a weakness in phonological processing speed. A weakness in this area can impact on the speed of retrieval of known information from the long-term memory.

---

[22] JCQ (20121) Access Arrangements and Reasonable Adjustments, 7.5.12, available at www.jcq.org.uk

- A test of working memory can evidence a weakness that can impact on the ability to perform mental calculations, retain what has been read and compose text.

- A test of reading efficiency can evidence a weakness that can impact on smooth and proficient reading.

Mathematical processing

A test of mathematical processing assesses the time taken to process mathematical concepts. This is sometimes called maths fluency. In such a test, the candidate is required to complete a series of, usually relatively simple, sums within strict time limits. Much like an assessment of reading fluency or efficiency, this measures how quickly and accurately the candidate can perform under timed conditions.

This is not the same as a timed assessment of maths attainment or maths computation, which is usually graded (it increases in difficulty), and where the focus is on mathematical knowledge rather than the candidate's fluency in performing maths tasks.

Some candidates have specific difficulties with speed of working in maths assessments and do not have difficulties in other types of examinations. Such a candidate will need 25% extra time in maths exams but will not require extra time in his other exams. In such cases, a below average score for mathematical fluency may be used as one of the two required measures for 25% extra time. Another score relating to a different area of speed of working which is below average (84 or less) or low average (85 – 89) will also need to be recorded within the 25% extra time section of Form 8 Part 2.

However, it is important to note that for a candidate who requires 25% extra time in maths exams, there is no requirement for a below average score in mathematical fluency to form part of the assessment evidence. It is perfectly acceptable to use two other measures relating to speed of working in the 25% extra time section of Form 8 Part 2.

Equally, a mathematical processing score cannot be used as assessment evidence for 25% extra time in examinations other than maths. Therefore, where a candidate requires 25% extra time in other subjects, even if they will also need the extra time in maths exams, the assessment evidence will need to include scores in two areas relating to speed of working other than mathematical processing.

Detailed Picture of Need

To accompany the fully completed Form 8, supplementary evidence known as the 'detailed picture of need' is required to support an application for 25% extra time for candidates with cognition and learning needs. This is additional centre-based evidence which is held on file to show the genuine need for the extra time. See Chapter 6 for full details.

Exceptional circumstances

In the vast majority of cases, the assessment evidence for a candidate requiring 25% extra time will include two below average scores or one below average score and one low average score in the areas discussed above.

For a candidate for whom there is extensive centre-based evidence showing the need for extra time, if a thorough investigation of these areas does not provide the necessary scores, it is possible to apply for 25% extra time on the basis of **two low average scores** (85 – 89) which relate to two different areas of speed of working.

The application will need to be referred to the relevant awarding bodies through Access Arrangements Online (see Chapter 14).

Rare and very exceptional circumstances

In a very few cases, the situation arises where there is extensive and detailed centre-based evidence for extra time for a candidate but a thorough investigation of the relevant assessment areas does not provide the required below average or low average scores.

25% extra time can be applied for if the following conditions are met, in addition to centre-based evidence showing an extensive history of need:

- The candidate would need to have a diagnostic assessment carried out (no earlier than Year 9) by a specialist diagnostic assessor (a specialist assessor who is qualified to conduct diagnostic assessments, such as an APC holder, or an HCPC registered psychologist).

- The assessment report must confirm a significant learning difficulty or disability.

- There must be a cluster of at least three standard scores in the 90 – 94 range relating to three different areas of speed of working. These must be recorded in Form 8 Part 2.

The application will need to be referred through Access Arrangements Online to the relevant awarding bodies, who may request evidence from the centre to justify the need for extra time. (See Chapter 14 for discussion of the application and referral process.)

Extra time of up to 50% (between 26% and 50% extra time)

Form 8 with assessment evidence is required for all candidates with cognition and learning needs who require more than 25% extra time. This includes those with an EHCP, IPD (Wales) or Statement of Special Educational Needs (Northern Ireland).

The assessment evidence for extra time of between 26% and 50% relates to the same areas as the evidence for 25% extra time: speed of reading, speed of writing and cognitive processing measures that have a substantial and long-term adverse effect on speed of working.

However, more than 25% extra time is considered to be an exceptional arrangement. There must be strong justification as to why a candidate with cognition and learning needs requires more than 25% extra time. For this reason, the following conditions need to be met[23]:

- A substantial body of centre-based evidence which justifies why more than 25% extra time is needed.

- At least two substantially below average scores (standard scores of 69 or below) relating to two different areas of speed of working recorded in Form 8 Part 2.

- The assessment must be conducted within 26 months of the final examination: approval is granted for 26 months from the assessment date and not from the application date. Once approval runs out, the evidence cannot be 'rolled forward'.

As with all 'exceptional' access arrangements, the application is not approved by the online system and must be referred, via AAO, to the awarding bodies who will consider each application on a case-by-case basis and make the decision as to whether the access arrangement is permitted.

Scribe

For a scribe (or one of the scribe options, see pages 46-47), Form 8 with assessment evidence is needed for candidates with cognition and learning needs who do not have an EHCP, IDP (Wales) or SEN Statement (Northern Ireland).

The areas that can provide assessment evidence for a scribe are, of course, connected with writing skills. They are:[24]

---

[23] JCQ (2021) Access Arrangements and Reasonable Adjustments, 5.3.2, available at www.jcq.org.uk
[24] JCQ (2021) Access Arrangements and Reasonable Adjustments, 7.5.11, available at www.jcq.org.uk

- A spelling accuracy score in the below average range (a standard score of 84 or less) with unrecognisable spelling attempts;
- A writing speed score in the below average range (a standard score of 84 or less).

In addition, the assessment can provide qualitative evidence of writing difficulties, where the writing is illegible or grammatically incomprehensible. These issues may not be evidenced by a standard score and as such will need to be referred to the awarding bodies for approval.

When assessing the need for a scribe, consider whether the candidate's difficulty with writing impacts on his ability to complete written responses. Equally, consider whether the written responses are likely to be able to be read by the examiner who is marking the paper.

Spelling

A low spelling score might be because of 'minor' errors, such as letter reversals (e.g. ie/ei reversals - *freinds*), incorrect double letters (e.g. *neccesary*), or homophones (words that sound the same but are spelt differently, e.g. *sweet, suite*). These types of spelling errors do not tend to impact on the ability to read and understand what has been written and so the candidate's writing remains readable for the examiner and can be marked.

However, in some cases a low score could be due to 'bizarre' spelling or very poor handwriting, both of which can make it extremely challenging to guess what each word might have been. These types of difficulties are likely to impact on the examiner's ability to read and mark what has been written.

Therefore, the assessment evidence in relation to spelling requires a below average score in which target words in the spelling assessment are unrecognisable and the assessor will need to make this qualitative judgement.

Within the candidate's writing, there might be additional evidence of poor spelling. However, this is not always the case as some candidates will only include in their own writing words that they feel confident they can spell. In addition, some candidates will spell accurately but will need time to consider their spellings as they write. In both cases, a weakness in spelling can impact on the quality (or speed) of their written communication despite spelling errors not being evident in the writing produced.

Writing speed

Measures of writing speed have already discussed in relation to the assessment evidence for 25% extra time (see pages 116 to 117). These same measures can provide assessment evidence for a scribe, where the standard score is below average (84 or less). The centre will need to determine whether the score is best used as evidence for a scribe or as one of the two measures for 25% extra time.

Where the writing speed score is to be used as assessment evidence for a scribe, it must be recorded in the scribe section of Form 8 Part 2.

In addition to the score for writing speed, a writing assessment of can provide qualitative evidence for a scribe:

Free writing which is illegible means that the handwriting is so poorly formed that it is indecipherable. If the work cannot be read due to legibility issues, it cannot be marked. Assessors and learning support teachers can be extremely adept at deciphering spelling and reading very poor handwriting - try to put yourself in the shoes of the busy examiner!

Free writing which is grammatically incomprehensible might be due to an overload of cognitive demands when a candidate is faced with writing, especially under timed conditions. Such a candidate may be better able to respond verbally than in writing (i.e. by dictating his responses to a scribe or using speech recognition software) or could require the support of the spell-check and grammar-check, and possibly the predictive text of a word processor.

Does a word processor solve the problem?

It is much preferred that the candidate works independently, so if the use of a word processor (as a centre-delegated access arrangement with spelling and grammar check switched off) meets the candidate's needs, this is the arrangement that should be put in place rather than a scribe.

Consider:

- Is the candidate proficient in the use of a word processor, meaning that it solves the issue of the poor legibility of written work?
- Does the use of a word processor mean that the candidate is able to draft and edit his work so that it makes sense?
- Does the use of a word processor improve the candidate's writing speed so that he is on an equal footing with others taking the exam?

Note: There is no standardised test of word-processed free writing, so an informal assessment can be made. The use of a word processor should reflect the candidate's normal way of working in the centre.

Language modifier

Form 8 with assessment evidence is needed for all candidates who require a language modifier, no matter which category of need their difficulties fall into and whether or not they have an EHCP, IDP (Wales) or Statement of SEN (Northern Ireland). This includes candidates who are deaf and those who have autism. For a candidate who is deaf, the assessment can be carried out by a qualified Teacher of the Deaf (ToD).

The following assessment evidence is needed:

- A standard score of 69 or less in relation to reading comprehension and/or vocabulary.[25]

The assessment must take place within 26 months of the final examination and approval is granted for 26 months from the assessment date and not from the application date. Once approval runs out, the evidence cannot be 'rolled forward'.

The extensive modification of language must reflect the candidate's normal way of working in the centre and all other arrangements, such as a reader, computer reader, and modified language papers (where available), should be considered before an LM is applied for.

Reading comprehension

A score for reading comprehension must relate to **reading comprehension of text or sentences**. The test can involve oral or silent reading and can be timed or untimed.

Vocabulary

A score for vocabulary can relate to an assessment **receptive vocabulary** which is usually assessed by the candidate selecting a picture that shows the meaning of a word spoken by the assessor, or **expressive vocabulary**, where the assessor says a word and the candidate has to say what it means.

As a LM is considered an 'exceptional' access arrangement, the application is not approved by the online system and must be referred, via AAO, to the awarding bodies who will consider each application on a case-by-case basis and make the decision as to whether the access arrangement is permitted.

---

[25] JCQ (2021) Access Arrangements and Reasonable Adjustments, 5.11.2, available at www.jcq.org.uk

Computer reader/reader

Although an online application must be made through Access Arrangements Online, Form 8 is not required for any candidate who requires a computer reader or reader, including those with cognition and learning needs. Therefore, no assessment evidence is needed to support an application for these arrangements.

Rather than Form 8, the SENCo or an equivalent member of staff in FE, produces a short concise file note to confirm that the candidate has persistent and significant reading difficulties (he is "disabled within the meaning of the Equality Act") and that there is a genuine need for the arrangement[26].

Whilst formal assessment evidence is not required and Form 8 is not used, some centres find it helpful to have assessment evidence of reading difficulties, evidenced by a below average score in reading. Various measures can be used, including:

Word reading
The assessment can measure the candidate's sight vocabulary (i.e. the words he is able to read automatically) as well as his decoding skills (his ability to apply sound/symbol knowledge) when tackling new words.

Significant weaknesses in word reading accuracy can impede access to written material and, in turn, impact on comprehension.

Reading comprehension
The test can involve oral or silent reading and can be timed or untimed.

A computer reader or reader can be helpful for a candidate who has reading comprehension difficulties as having the text read aloud can aid processing and understanding of text. A learner who has reading difficulties is able to focus on the meaning of the words without the additional burden of having to read independently.

Reading speed
A candidate with centre-based evidence of reading difficulties may have competent reading accuracy and comprehension but take longer than expected to decode the words, leading to a below average score for reading speed (or rate or fluency) or may need to re-read text several times to process it and absorb its meaning, leading to a below average score for reading comprehension speed.

The centre-based evidence will help the SENCo to determine whether 25% extra time or a computer reader/reader is the best arrangement for a candidate with slow reading speed.

---

[26] JCQ (2021) Access Arrangements and Reasonable Adjustments, 5.5.5, available at www.jcq.org.uk

10. Test Choices: Tests available for use in access arrangements assessments

The following tests are available currently and can provide assessment evidence for access arrangements. The tables are organised in the same order as JCQ Form 8 Part 2 (see Chapter 11). Some tests will appear in more than one list as they include assessments in a range of areas.

It is important to remember that this is not a prescribed list of tests. Other tests may be available that can also provide assessment evidence for access arrangements. Closed Tests (available to registered or chartered psychologists only) have not been included in the lists.

Assessment evidence for extra time

Reading speed (continuous text)

Measures of reading speed (continuous text) can include reading rate, reading fluency and reading comprehension speed.

Test	Ceiling age	Publisher & year	Notes
Academic Achievement Battery (AAB)	85.11	PAR, Inc 2014	Reading Fluency subtest Oral reading of text (1 passage)
Adult Reading Test Second Edition (ART-2)	55.11	Pearson Assessment 2016	Silent and Oral subtests Reading rate measure included within reading comprehension UK norms from FE and HE students For use from 16+
Diagnostic Reading Analysis Third Edition (DRA-3)	16.08	Hodder Education 2019	Oral reading rate within text-level reading comprehension Comprehension processing speed UK norms Use year group norms (not age-based)
Dyslexia Portfolio	15.11	GL Assessment 2008	Reading Speed subtest Silent or oral reading of sentences Examinee marks 'yes/no' to a series of sentences.
Feifer Assessment of Reading (FAR)	21.11	PAR, Inc 2015	Two subtests: Silent Reading Fluency, Oral Reading Fluency

Test	Ceiling age	Publisher & year	Notes
Exact	24.11	GL Assessment 2009	UK norms Computer-based administration and scoring Reading Comprehension Speed measured within reading comprehension Group testing possible
Gray Oral Reading Tests 5th Edition (GORT-5)	23.11	PRO ED, Inc 2012	Oral reading at text-level Rate and Fluency measures included within reading comprehension
Kaufman Test of Educational Achievement 3rd Edition (KTEA-3)	25.11	Pearson Assessment 2014	Silent Reading Fluency subtest Mark 'yes/no' answer to a series of written questions in 2-minute time limit Two parallel forms purchased separately
SPaRCS Test	18.11	Education Elephant 2017	Reading Comprehension Speed subtest Multiple choice Group testing possible UK (NI) and ROI norms
Wechsler Individual Achievement Test 3rd UK Edition (WIAT-III UK)	25.11	Pearson Assessment 2017	Oral Reading Fluency subtest UK norms Can be purchased and used by APC holders
Wechsler Individual Achievement Test 3rd UK Edition for Teachers (WIAT-III UK-T)	25.11	Pearson Assessment 2018	Oral Reading Fluency subtest UK norms
Woodcock Reading Mastery Tests 3rd Edition (WRMT-III)	79.11	Pearson Assessment 2011	Oral Reading Fluency subtest 2 parallel forms
Woodcock-Johnson IV Tests of Achievement (WJ IV ACH) UK and Ireland edition	90+	Riverside Insights 2014	Sentence Reading Fluency subtest Mark 'yes/no' answer to a series of written questions 3-minute time limit Online scoring platform (purchase credits)
York Assessment of Reading for Comprehension Secondary (YARC)	16.11	GL Assessment 2010	Reading Rate (oral) and Fluency measured within reading comprehension UK norms

Writing Speed

Measures of writing speed require the candidate to write by hand and can include free writing, writing fluency, writing to dictation or a composite score for writing speed. A test of writing speed can provide assessment evidence for either 25% extra time (for a candidate who writes by hand in examinations) or for a scribe.

Test	Ceiling age	Publisher & year	Notes
Detailed Assessment of Speed of Handwriting (DASH)	16.11	Pearson Assessment 2007	Use either Free Writing subtest or Total Handwriting Speed composite Convert FW subtest scaled score to standard score UK norms
Detailed Assessment of Speed of Handwriting 17+ (DASH 17+)	25.11	Pearson Assessment 2010	Use either Free Writing subtest or Total Handwriting Speed composite Convert FW subtest scaled score to standard score UK norms
Dyslexia Portfolio	15.11	GL Assessment 2008	Rate of Writing: Candidate completes sentences within a 5-minute time limit UK norms
Exact	24.11	GL Assessment 2009	Writing to dictation. Computer-based although subtest is handwritten. (Note: Typing subtest cannot be used) UK norms
Kaufman Test of Educational Achievement 3rd Edition (KTEA-3)	25.11	Pearson Assessment 2014	Writing Fluency subtest: Candidate writes a short sentence for each picture within a 5-minute time limit Two forms purchased separately
Woodcock-Johnson IV Tests of Achievement (WJ IV ACH) UK and Ireland edition	90+	Riverside Insights 2014	Sentence Writing Fluency subtest Candidate writes a sentence for each picture which includes 3 stimulus words 5-minute time limit Online scoring platform (purchase credits)

Cognitive Processing

Measures of cognitive processing will impact of speed of working and can include phonological processing, short term/working memory, visual and visual-motor processing, and other tests measuring the fluency and efficiency of performing cognitive tasks. A test of mathematical processing can provide evidence for extra time in maths exams only.

Test	Ceiling age	Publisher & year	Notes
Academic Achievement Battery (AAB)	85.11	PAR, Inc 2014	Oral Fluency subtest
Beery-Buktenica Developmental Test of Visual-Motor Integration 6th Edition (Beery VMI)	100.11	Pearson Assessment 2010	Measures of: Visual-motor integration Visual perception Motor coordination Group testing possible
Comprehensive Test of Phonological Processing 2nd Edition (CTOPP2)	24.11	PRO-ED, Inc 2013	9 subtests making 4 composites Composites are: Phonological Awareness (3 subtests) Phonological Memory (2 subtests) Rapid Symbolic Naming – a measure of phonological processing speed (2 subtests) Alternate Phonological Awareness (2 subtests)
Developmental Test of Visual Perception-Adolescent and Adult: Second Edition (DTVP-A:2)	74.11	PRO-ED, Inc 2021	7 subtests and 4 indexes measuring visual perception and visual-motor difficulties Online scoring only
Dyslexia Portfolio	15.11	GL Assessment 2008	Measures of: Phoneme Deletion Nonword Reading Naming Speed Recall of Digits Forwards Recall of Digits Backwards
Feifer Assessment of Mathematics (FAM)	21.11	PAR, Inc 2015	Four measures of Maths Fluency: Addition Fluency Subtraction Fluency Multiplication Fluency Division Fluency Evidence for 25% in maths exams only

Test	Ceiling age	Publisher & year	Notes
Feifer Assessment of Reading (FAR)	21.11	PAR, Inc 2015	Measures of: Phonemic Awareness Isolated and Irregular Word Reading Fluency Positioning Sounds Visual Perception Rapid Automatic Naming Orthographical and Morphological Processing
Full Range Test of Visual Motor Integration (FRTVMI)	74.11	PRO-ED, Inc 2005	Measures visual-motor skills through design copying tasks
Kaufman Test of Educational Achievement 3rd Edition (KTEA-3)	25.11	Pearson Assessment 2014	Measures of: Phonological Processing Maths Fluency (Evidence for 25% in maths exams only) Associational Fluency Object Naming Facility Letter Naming Facility Word Recognition Fluency Decoding Fluency
Rapid Automatized Naming and Rapid Alternating Stimulus Tests (RAN/RAS)	18.11	PRO-ED, Inc 2005	6 measures of Rapid Naming including Objects, Colours, Numbers, Letters, 2-Set Letters and Numbers, 3-Set Letters, Numbers and Colours
Recall (Second edition)	16.11	GL Assessment 2015	Computer-based administration and scoring 3 subtests assessing working memory: Phonological Loop, Visuo-spatial Sketchpad, Central Executive Function 2 composite scores: Composite Working Memory Skills, Working Memory Processing Speed UK norms
SPaRCS Test	18.11	Education Elephant 2017	Processing Speed (number-letter matching) Group testing possible UK (NI) and ROI norms
Symbol Digit Modalities Test (SDMT)	78.11	Western Psychological Services 1973	Coding test (visual processing) Written and oral subtests Group testing possible

Test	Ceiling age	Publisher & year	Notes
TAPS-4 A Language Processing Skills Assessment	21.11	American Therapy Publications 2018	Phonological Processing Index – 4 subtests administered via CD Auditory Memory Index – 4 subtests administered verbally
Test of Information Processing Skills (TIPS)	80+	American Therapy Publications 2009	Measures of short-term/working memory: Visual Ordered and Unordered & Auditory Ordered and Unordered Indexes
Test of Memory and Learning 2nd Edition (TOMAL-2)	59.11	Pearson Assessment 2007	Measures of short-term/working memory including: Attention/Concentration Index – 4 verbal subtests and 1 visual subtest
Test of Silent Word Reading Fluency: Second Edition (TOSWRF2)	24.11	PRO-ED, Inc 2014	Candidates draw lines to demarcate word boundaries 3-minute time limit parallel forms
Test of Visual-Motor Skills 3rd Edition (TVMS-3)	90+	American Therapy Publications 2010	Measures visual-motor skills through design copying tasks
Test of Word Reading Efficiency 2nd Edition (TOWRE-2)	24.11	PRO-ED, Inc 2012	Total Word Reading Efficiency composite from 2 subtests: Sight Word Efficiency Phonemic Decoding Efficiency
Wechsler Individual Achievement Test 3rd UK Edition (WIAT-III UK)	25.11	Pearson Assessment 2017	Maths Fluency subtest (Evidence for 25% in maths exams only) UK norms Can be purchased and used by APC holders
Wide Range Assessment of Memory and Learning 2nd Edition (WRAML2)	90.11	Pearson Assessment 2003	Measures of short-term/working memory including: Attention/Concentration Index (2 subtests) Working Memory Index (2 subtests)
Woodcock-Johnson IV Tests of Achievement (WJ IV ACH) UK and Ireland edition	90	Riverside Insights 2014	Maths Facts Fluency subtest (Evidence for 25% in maths exams only) Online scoring platform (purchase credits)

Test	Ceiling age	Publisher & year	Notes
Woodcock-Johnson IV Tests of Cognitive Abilities (WJ IV COG)	90+	Riverside Insights 2014	Measures of cognitive processing including: Short-term Working Memory Cluster – 3 tests; Auditory Processing Cluster – 2 tests; Cognitive Processing Speed Cluster – 2 tests Online scoring platform (purchase credits) Can be purchased and used by APC holders

Assessment evidence for a scribe

Spelling

A standalone measure of spelling accuracy at word level can provide evidence for a scribe where there are unrecognisable spelling attempts.

Test	Ceiling age	Publisher & year	Notes
Academic Achievement Battery (AAB)	85.11	PAR, Inc 2014	US Grade-based start points
Diagnostic Spelling Tests 4 and 5	4: 14 5: 20+	Hodder Education 2006	Photocopiable test form 2 parallel forms UK norms
Dyslexia Portfolio	15.11	GL Assessment 2008	UK norms Computer-based scoring
Exact	24	2009	Computer-based administration and scoring: Candidate types answers UK norms
Helen Arkell Spelling Test Version 2 (HAST-2)	59.11	Helen Arkell Dyslexia Centre 2012	Photocopiable test form 2 parallel forms (A and B) 1 additional combined form (C) UK norms
Kaufman Test of Educational Achievement 3rd Edition (KTEA-3)	25.11	Pearson Assessment 2014	Two forms purchased separately

Test	Ceiling age	Publisher & year	Notes
Single Word Spelling Test (SWST)	14	GL Assessment 2007	UK norms Digital & paper versions
SPaRCS Test	18.11	Education Elephant 2017	UK (NI) and ROI norms
Vernon Graded Word Spelling Test – 3rd Edition	18+	Hodder Education 2006	UK norms
Wechsler Individual Achievement Test 3rd UK Edition (WIAT-III UK)	25.11	Pearson Assessment 2017	UK norms Can be purchased and used by APC holders
Wechsler Individual Achievement Test 3rd UK Edition for Teachers (WIAT-III-UK-T)	25.11	Pearson Assessment 2018	UK norms
Wide Range Achievement Test 5 (WRAT5)	85+	Pearson Assessment 2017	Paper-based and on-screen versions
Woodcock-Johnson IV Tests of Achievement (WJ IV ACH) UK and Ireland edition	90	Riverside Insights 2014	Online scoring platform (purchase credits)

Writing Speed

Measures of writing speed require the candidate to write by hand and can include free writing, writing fluency, writing to dictation or a composite score for writing speed.

Handwriting can also be analysed qualitatively for legibility and grammatical comprehensibility.

The writing speed tests listed on page 127 can provide assessment evidence for a scribe with the assessment data recorded in the Scribe section of Form 8 Part 2.

Assessment evidence for a language modifier

Reading comprehension

Measures of reading comprehension at text or sentence level can be used to evidence the need for a language modifier.

Test	Ceiling age	Publisher & year	Notes
Academic Achievement Battery (AAB)	85.11	PAR, Inc 2014	Sentence marking using three passages
Access Reading Tests 3rd Edition (ART-3)	25.11	Hodder Education 2018	Multiple choice Group testing possible UK norms Four parallel forms Paper and digital versions
Adult Reading Test 2 (ART-2)	55.11	Pearson Assessment 2016	Silent and Oral subtests Verbal questions and responses UK norms from FE and HE students For use from 16+
Diagnostic Reading Analysis 3rd Edition (DRA-3)	16.08	Hodder Education 2019	Oral reading at text-level 2 parallel forms UK norms Use year group norms (not aged-based)
Exact	24	GL Assessment 2009	Computer-based administration and scoring Multiple choice 2 parallel forms UK norms Group testing possible
Feifer Assessment of Reading (FAR)	21.11	PAR, Inc. 2015	Silent Reading Fluency - Comprehension (SRF-C) Silent reading at text level Candidate answers comprehension questions without referring back to text
Gray Oral Reading Tests 5th Edition (GORT-5)	23.11	PRO-ED, Inc. 2012	Oral reading at text-level Verbal questions and responses without referring back to text
Gray Silent Reading Tests (GSRT)	25.11	PRO-ED, Inc. 2000	Silent reading Multiple choice 2 parallel forms

Test	Ceiling age	Publisher & year	Notes
Hodder Group Reading Test Second Edition (HGRT-II) Test 3	16+	Hodder Education 2007	Multiple choice, sentence and text completion 2 parallel forms UK norms Restricted to schools and institutions only
Kaufman Test of Educational Achievement 3rd Edition (KTEA-3)	25.11	Pearson Assessment 2014	Text-level (oral or silent) Written questions, oral responses Two forms purchased separately
New Group Reading Test (NGRT) 3rd Edition	16	GL Assessment 2010	3 equivalent forms Paper and digital versions Sentence completion and passage comprehension UK norms
Suffolk Reading Scale Digital (SRS Digital) Level 4	16.11	GL Assessment 2007	Multiple choice sentence completion Digital administration and scoring UK norms
Wechsler Individual Achievement Test 3rd UK Edition (WIAT-III UK)	25.11	Pearson Assessment 2017	Text-level (oral or silent) Verbal questions and responses UK norms Can be purchased and used by APC holders
Wechsler Individual Achievement Test 3rd UK Edition for Teachers (WIAT-III-UK-T)	25.11	Pearson Assessment 2018	Text-level (oral or silent) Verbal questions and responses UK norms
Wide Range Achievement Test 5 (WRAT5)	85+	Pearson Assessment 2017	Sentence-level (oral or silent) Candidate provides words to complete sentences 2 parallel forms Paper-based and digital versions
Wide Range Achievement Test – Expanded (WRAT-E) Group Form Level 5	24.11	Pearson Assessment 2000	Text level reading comprehension
Wide Range Achievement Test – Expanded (WRAT-E) Individual Form	18.11	Pearson Assessment 2000	Silent reading comprehension

Test	Ceiling age	Publisher & year	Notes
Woodcock-Johnson IV Tests of Achievement (WJ IV ACH) UK and Ireland edition	90	Riverside Insights 2014	Silent reading at text-level Candidate provides words to complete sentences Online scoring platform (purchase credits)
Woodcock Reading Mastery Tests 3rd Edition (WRMT-III)	79.11	Pearson Assessment 2011	Silent passage comprehension 2 parallel forms
York Assessment of Reading for Comprehension Secondary (YARC)	16.11	GL Assessment 2010	Oral reading at text-level UK norms

Vocabulary

Measures of vocabulary to evidence the need for a language modifier can include tests of receptive and expressive vocabulary.

Test	Ceiling age	Publisher & year	Notes
British Picture Vocabulary Scale 3rd Edition (BPVS-III)	16.11	GL Assessment 2009	Receptive language UK norms
Expressive Vocabulary Test 3nrd Edition (EVT-3)	90	Pearson Assessment 2019	Expressive vocabulary and word retrieval 2 parallel forms Hand or digital scoring
Peabody Picture Vocabulary Test 5th Edition (PPVT-5)	90+	Pearson Assessment 2018	Receptive vocabulary acquisition Co-normed with EVT-3 Hand or digital scoring
Ravens 2 Progressive Matrices (Mill Hill Vocabulary Scale - MHV)	18	Pearson Assessment 2008	Mill Hill Vocabulary Scale Individual or group administration UK norms
Vocabulary Assessment Scales-Expressive and Vocabulary Assessment Scales-Receptive (VAS-E, VAS-R)	95	PAR, Inc 2013	Picture vocabulary test assessing expressive and receptive language 2 subtest scores and 1 composite

Test	Ceiling age	Publisher & year	Notes
Wide Range Intelligence Test (WRIT)	84.11	Pearson Assessment 2000	2 subtests - Vocabulary and Verbal Analogies Verbal Ability composite
Woodcock-Johnson IV Tests of Cognitive Abilities (WJ IV COG)	90+	Riverside Insights 2014	Oral Vocabulary Online scoring platform (purchase credits) Can be purchased and used by APC holders

Remember, the test lists above are not exhaustive. Assessors should also be aware that new tests are published on a regular basis and older tests can be withdrawn from use.

Where possible, the most recent edition of a test should be used. (See Chapters 7 and 8 for further discussion on selecting appropriate tests.)

Check publishers' websites for details of tests. Some suppliers include information about which of their tests can be used for access arrangements and the evidence that they provide. Whilst this is useful, it is important to consider each test against the current JCQ criteria to ensure that the information reflects up-to-date guidance.

Another useful source of information about standardised tests is the website of the SpLD Assessment Standards Committee (SASC). SASC is a standard-setting group concerned with the diagnostic assessment of specific learning difficulties. The organisation is responsible for overseeing and approving processes of awarding SpLD Assessment Practising Certificates.

Within SASC, the SpLD Test Evaluation Committee (STEC) reviews test resources and publishes assessment guidance on the SASC website. It also maintains lists of approved assessment materials for SpLDs.[27] There are test lists for assessments of pre-16 learners and post-16 learners and these are updated periodically.

---

[27] STEC test lists, reviews and information can be found on the SASC website: www.sasc.org.uk

11. Recording and Reporting Assessment Outcomes: Form 8 Part 2

JCQ Form 8 Part 2 is used to record the assessment data that provides evidence for access arrangements; it is 'the access arrangements assessment report'.

Reports

The 'diagnostic assessment report'

A 'diagnostic assessment' investigates the cognitive and attainment profile of an individual in order to diagnose, identify or confirm a specific learning difficulty (SpLD). The report includes detailed analysis of performance and gives recommendations for the learner.

HCPC registered psychologists and specialist assessors holding an SpLD Assessment Practising Certificate (APC), or a qualification at APC level, are able to carry out diagnostic assessments.

This type of assessment is required to support an application for the Disabled Students Allowance (DSA) in Higher Education.

The 'access arrangements assessment report'

Form 8 is the access arrangements assessment report. Part 1 contains the background information from the centre, qualifying test scores are recorded within Part 2, and Part 3 lists the access arrangements requiring approval.

An assessment in the context of access arrangements is more limited than a diagnostic assessment as it does not require a diagnosis of a SpLD – just confirmation that a difficulty in learning exists: specifically, a difficulty that affects performance in examinations and assessments. The assessor needs only to select those tests that are necessary to show the difficulties experienced by the candidate (guided by the centre evidence).

Professionals should make students and/or parents aware that, on its own, Form 8 does not constitute an identification of a SpLD and that a referral for further testing will be needed to secure a diagnosis, should this be required.

The standard, format and type of evidence to be presented in an access arrangements assessment report need to be consistent. Assessors conducting assessments and SENCos reporting the centre evidence and making the final decisions on which access arrangements are provided must be scrupulous in the standards they apply. They must be comfortable that these would stand up to scrutiny if challenged by JCQ inspectors, learners and their parents and other professionals. Therefore, it is essential that the correct evidence is obtained and retained for every access arrangements application.

The evidence must be presented to JCQ Centre Inspectors in the prescribed format. This enables inspectors, who are not trained in standardised assessment, to see at a glance whether the correct assessment evidence has been obtained. The uniform presentation of the data will also be helpful when making the online applications, as the required centre-based and assessment information will be together on one form and easily accessible.

From the JCQ's perspective, access arrangements assessors are not required to make direct recommendations about support or, indeed, whether a candidate should be entered for particular examinations. The assessor's role is to contribute evidence of learning difficulties. This takes professional skill and judgement, particularly in less obvious cases.

Summary Table of Results

The access arrangements assessor need only supply assessment information within Form 8 Part 2 that supports an application for access arrangements. However, best practice is to explore the candidate's profile using a range of assessment tools, particularly were the candidate requires 25% extra time as two scores are needed in different areas relating to speed of working. The assessment results may include scores that do not fulfil the JCQ assessment criteria. It can, therefore, be helpful to provide a summary table of results containing all the scores from the range of assessments that were carried out with a learner.

There are various formats that the table of results can take but it is helpful if they are produced on a single page, providing an 'at a glance' summary of the assessment data. The following pages contain examples of useful formats for presenting assessment results (also see Appendix 2 for online resources). Simple spreadsheets can also be devised that allow the assessor to input test scores and produce a table or chart of the results.

These tables of results are an optional, but useful, accompaniment to JCQ Form 8 Part 2; they do not replace it. They can be a convenient way of feeding back the results of the assessment to the student or parents. They also show the spread of a student's scores. The access arrangements assessment, by its very nature, tends to focus on the areas of difficulty for a student. If the scores in some areas of assessment are mid-average or above, they will not be included on Form 8 Part 2 as they do not contribute assessment evidence for access arrangements. Showing these higher scores within a table of results means that the strengths can be discussed and celebrated. However, it should be remembered that measures of underlying ability (which may be an area of strength for the candidate) are not used in an assessment for access arrangements. Only fully qualified assessors can use such tests and, in usual circumstances, they are administered as part of a diagnostic assessment.

Information gained from an assessment could be used to inform an IEP or support plan or added to a learner's pen portrait. It may also provide clues to support strategies that the learner can be encouraged and supported to develop and use. For example, if the profile of scores indicates strengths in visual memory or visual processing, with weaker verbal memory and phonological processing, approaches to revision and learning incorporating visual strategies could be discussed and explored.

Assessment for Access Arrangements:

Summary of results on standardised tests

Name:

Age:

Date of Birth:

Date tested:

Standard Deviation	-3	-2	-1	0	+1	+2	+3
Standardised scores	Below 70	70 - 84	85	100	115	116 - 130	131+
Level descriptor	well below	below average	low	average range	high	above average	well above

Observations/notes

Patoss: This sheet can be photocopied without infringing copyright

Summary Table of Results

Name of Test	Assessment evidence for?	Standard Score	Range
E.g. *Academic Achievement Battery (AAB) Fluency*	*25% Extra time*	*75*	*Below average*

Observations/notes

Patoss: This sheet can be photocopied without infringing copyright

Charts can be made using Excel to help display this information visually to accompany assessment records.

Two examples are shown below. Templates are included in the downloadable resources accompanying this Guide (see Appendix 2).

Excel spreadsheet 1:
The spreadsheet is set up so that test names and scores are added in the left-hand column. Test names will then appear in a list on the chart, with a mark to show the standard score. The chart is designed to fit onto an A4 page, for printing.

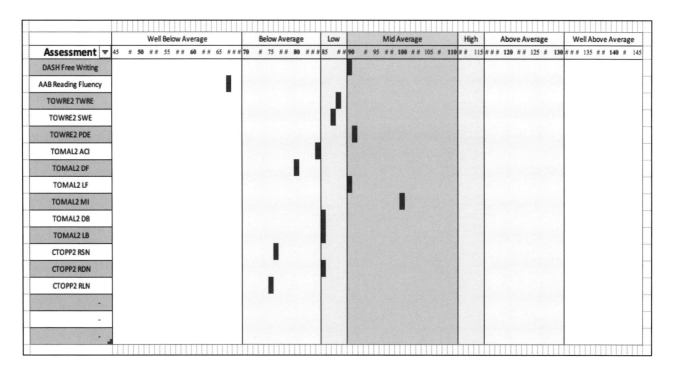

This example shows a completed chart.

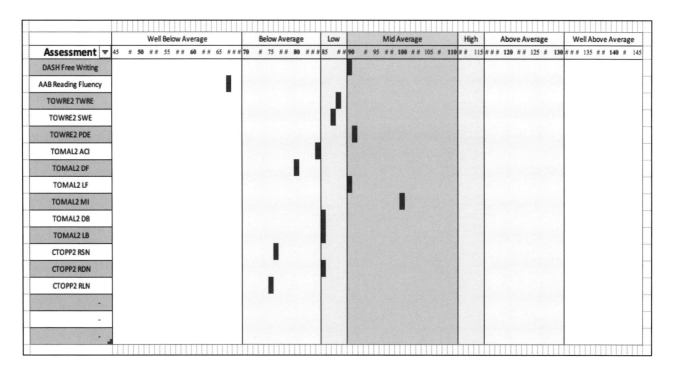

Excel spreadsheet 2:

This time, the spreadsheet is set up to produce a bar chart of standard scores. The upper and lower limits of the graph can be adjusted each time, so that they are set 10 points above and below the highest and lowest scores. Markers for the average range have been added. The chart can be set to a horizontal or vertical view.

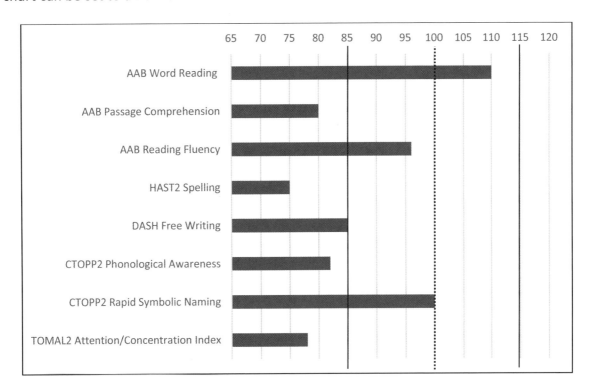

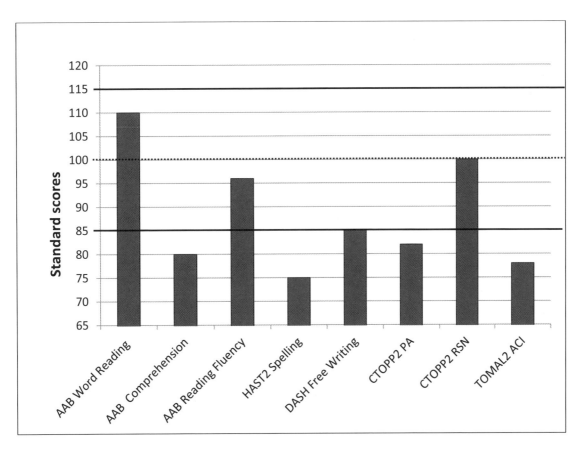

Completing Form 8 Part 2

In Chapter 9, the JCQ assessment criteria were discussed in relation to Form 8 Part 2.

The following pages will take you through the completion of Form 8 Part 2. A guidance sheet for completing Form 8 is available on the Patoss website as a downloadable resource to accompany this book (see Appendix 2).

A box for the candidate's name can be found at the top right of every page. Ensure that each of these is completed.

Part 2	Candidate's name:

Guidance information is provided at the top of Part 2, to help in the completion of the form. Assessors are signposted to information within the JCQ AARA document. Chapter 7 is the section of the regulations concerning learning difficulties and provides information about who is qualified to assess for access arrangements. Guidance on completing of Form 8 Part 2 can be found there.

This part must be completed by the qualified assessor (see section 7.3 of the JCQ publication *Access Arrangements and Reasonable Adjustments*) **after receiving a completed Part 1 from the SENCo.** The assessor is not required to recommend access arrangements but to assess the candidate and discuss appropriate arrangements with the SENCo.

Use the guidance notes in Chapter 7 of the JCQ publication *Access Arrangements and Reasonable Adjustments* to complete this form.

Complete those sections necessary to support the application, e.g. sections on speed of working for 25% extra time. Do not delete sections or amend the wording on the form. **Please insert 'n/a' in the top line of boxes not completed.**

The bottom paragraph clarifies that it may not be necessary to complete every section of Part 2. The assessor need only complete the boxes that provide assessment evidence for access arrangements. Scores that do not provide assessment evidence (i.e. because they are not below average, or low average in some cases, do not need to be included.)

If the assessor is not including assessment evidence in a box or section, 'n/a' should be added to the first line of the box to show that it has been left uncompleted deliberately and has not been missed in error.

The assessment evidence in Form 8 Part 2 is organised into three sections: 'Evidence for 25% extra time', 'Evidence for a scribe', and 'Other relevant information'. The evidence requirements for each arrangement are set out at the start of each section.

In the 25% extra time and scribe sections, there are separate boxes for the various assessment areas that can provide assessment evidence. For 25% extra time, there are boxes for assessments of reading speed, writing speed and cognitive processing.

To accompany each test result box, there are one or more questions to be answered. Make sure that you read the questions carefully so that the assessment information is provided correctly.

If you are not including evidence for the assessment area, the question can be left unanswered.

To answer the question, you need to check the relevant box. Double-clicking in the box should bring up a 'check box form'. You can then click the 'Ticked' field to add a cross to the relevant box. See illustrations below.

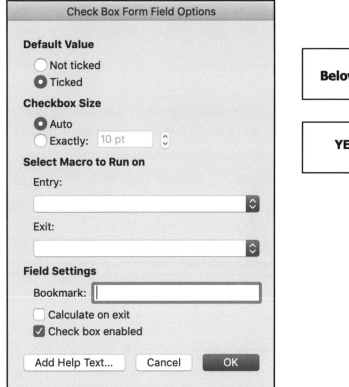

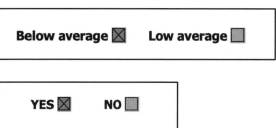

If you are not including a test score for the assessment area, write, "n/a" in the first row of the box and move on.

Name of test (and subtest)	n/a
Test ceiling	
Date of administration	
Standardised score	

If you are including a score, make sure to complete each row of the box.

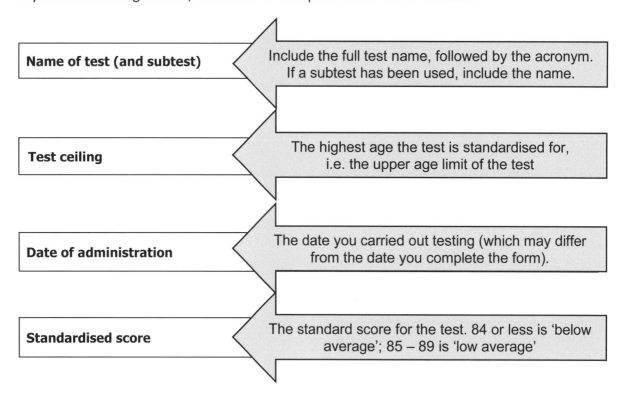

Name of test (and subtest) — Include the full test name, followed by the acronym. If a subtest has been used, include the name.

Test ceiling — The highest age the test is standardised for, i.e. the upper age limit of the test

Date of administration — The date you carried out testing (which may differ from the date you complete the form).

Standardised score — The standard score for the test. 84 or less is 'below average'; 85 – 89 is 'low average'

25% extra time

At the start of the 25% extra time section of Form 8, there are references to sections of the JCQ AARA document that provide information on assessments of reading speed, writing speed and cognitive processing.

Evidence for 25% extra time

For candidates requiring extra time, assessment evidence must relate to at least two different areas of speed of working (see sections 5.2.2, 7.5.10, 7.5.11 and 7.5.12 of the JCQ publication *Access Arrangements and Reasonable Adjustments*)

For each area of testing, you are asked whether there are scores that are below average (standard scores below 85) or low average (standard scores between 85 and 89). If you have relevant scores, check the box to indicate this.

The first box for 25% extra time evidence elates to reading speed. This must come from a test measuring the speed of reading continuous text (not isolated words).

Reading speed (continuous text)

Does the candidate read continuous text at a speed which is **below average** (a standard score of 84 or less) or **low average** (a standard score of 85 to 89)?

Below average ▨   Low average ▨

The second is for writing speed. An assessment of writing speed can provide evidence for either 25% extra time (where a candidate writes by hand) or a scribe. Make sure that you record the score in the correct box, depending on which access arrangement it will provide evidence for.

For 25% extra time, the only question to answer in relation to writing speed is whether the score is below average or low average.

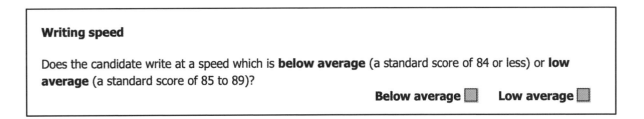

Writing speed

Does the candidate write at a speed which is **below average** (a standard score of 84 or less) or **low average** (a standard score of 85 to 89)?

Below average ☐   Low average ☐

The final box in which to record assessment evidence for 25% extra time relates to measures of cognitive processing. The test results box includes two columns so that results from two different areas of processing can be included.

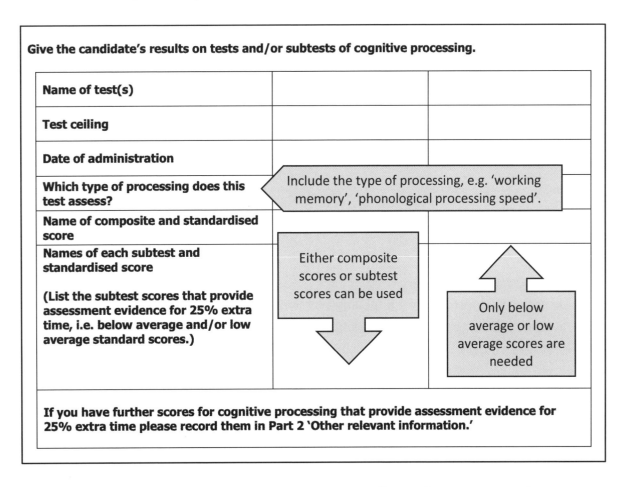

Give the candidate's results on tests and/or subtests of cognitive processing.		
Name of test(s)		
Test ceiling		
Date of administration		
Which type of processing does this test assess?	Include the type of processing, e.g. 'working memory', 'phonological processing speed'.	
Name of composite and standardised score		
Names of each subtest and standardised score (List the subtest scores that provide assessment evidence for 25% extra time, i.e. below average and/or low average standard scores.)	Either composite scores or subtest scores can be used	Only below average or low average scores are needed
If you have further scores for cognitive processing that provide assessment evidence for 25% extra time please record them in Part 2 'Other relevant information.'		

A completed example is shown on the next page. You will note that not every subtest score that makes up the composite has been included. Only below average and low average scores need to be recorded. Equally, if the composite score does not provide evidence, there is no need to include it. Scores that do not provide assessment evidence can be left off the form.

Name of test(s)	Comprehensive Test of Phonological Processing Second Edition (CTOPP2)	Test of Memory and Learning Second Edition (TOMAL2)
Test ceiling	24.11	59.11
Date of administration	02.09.XX	02.09.XX
Which type of processing does this test assess?	Phonological processing speed	Short term/working memory
Name of composite and standardised score	Rapid Symbolic Naming 82	Attention/Concentration Index 88
Names of each subtest and standardised score **(List the subtest scores that provide assessment evidence for 25% extra time, i.e. below average and/or low average standard scores.)**	Rapid Digit Naming 85 Rapid Letter Naming 85	Digits Forward 80

Example (note: subtest scaled scores are converted to standard scores)

If you have further scores for cognitive processing that provide assessment evidence for 25% extra time please record them in Part 2 'Other relevant information.'

Scribe

The scribe section of Form 8 Part 2 includes boxes to record assessment evidence relating to writing skills: spelling and writing speed.

Spelling

Is the candidate's spelling accuracy in the **below average range** (a standard score of 84 or less) with unrecognisable spelling attempts?

YES ☐   NO ☐

The accompanying question for the spelling assessment asks whether spelling accuracy is below average with unrecognisable spelling attempts. To answer, 'yes' both elements must be present (see Chapter 9 for further discussion).

In relation to an assessment of writing skills, there are three questions on the form which tie in with the assessment criteria for a scribe (see Chapter 9). As with the question above, which asks about unrecognisable spelling attempts, the assessor needs to use qualitative judgements when answering the first two questions as there are no scores associated with the quality and legibility of writing.

Writing

Is the candidate's writing grammatically incomprehensible to someone who is not familiar with it?

YES ☐   NO ☐

Does the candidate's handwriting render his or her writing largely illegible to someone who is not familiar with it?

YES ☐   NO ☐

Is the candidate's writing speed in the **below average range**? (a standard score of 84 or less)

YES ☐   NO ☐

A further box is provided in Part 2 for **Other relevant information**. Here, the assessment evidence for 26% to 50% extra time and for a language modifier can be recorded. The evidence requirements are provided at the top of the box, along with references to more detailed information in the AARA document. Any additional scores for 25% extra time, such as further processing scores, can also be added here.

For an adult learner who is aged 25 or over, a test may have been used for which the candidate's age is above the test ceiling age. This should also be explained in this Other relevant information box (see pages 97 to 98).

Other relevant information

Evidence for 26% to 50% extra time or a Language Modifier

Record all additional assessment evidence which is relevant to the access arrangement(s) required by the candidate. For each test, include the **name of test/subtest, test ceiling, date of assessment, area assessed and standardised score**.

For candidates requiring **extra time of up to 50%** (26% to 50% extra time) **two** very substantially below average standardised scores relating to **two different areas of speed of working** are required – two standard scores of 69 or less.

For candidates requiring **a Language Modifier** a standard score of 69 or less is required in relation to reading comprehension and/or vocabulary.

A standard score of 69 or less is two standard deviations below the mean on a nationally standardised test. (See **sections 5.3 and 5.11** of the JCQ publication *Access Arrangements and Reasonable Adjustments*.)

The final page of Part 2 needs careful completion to ensure that your information, as the assessor who has conducted the tests that are recorded in Part 2, is accurate.

Once completed, Form 8 Part 2 should be given to the SENCo so that it can be considered along with the centre-based evidence to make the final decision on which access arrangements are to be applied for and Part 3 can be completed.

Name of the assessor who carried out all of the tests recorded in Part 2, as approved by the head of centre

_____

(Please print)

> Your name, as the assessor, goes here.

Are you:

an appropriately qualified psychologist registered with the Health & Care Professions Council?   **YES** ☐   **NO** ☐

Unique registration number _____

a specialist assessor with a **current** SpLD Assessment Practising Certificate?   **YES** ☐   **NO** ☐

APC number as listed on the SASC website _____

an access arrangements assessor who has **successfully completed a post-graduate course at or equivalent to Level 7, including at least 100 hours relating to individual specialist assessment**?

YES ☐   **NO** ☐

> Indicate which of the 3 types of qualification you hold, and your HCPC or APC number.

Specialist qualification held.........................

Name of awarding body..............................

> Provide the exact details of the name of your qualification and awarding body.

I certify that the above information is accurate and that I carried out **all the assessments** recorded in Part 2.

(It is not acceptable for an assessor to sign if they have not carried out all the tests recorded in Part 2 of this form.)

Signature†   Date |
---   --

†A signed copy of Form 8 **must** be retained on file by the SENCo for inspection purposes to support an approved application processed on-line (**see page 1 for the list of qualifications**).

A handwritten, electronic or typed signature is acceptable.

> Make sure to sign and date the form. In doing so, you are confirming that you, personally, have carried out all the tests recorded within Form 8 Part 2.
>
> It is not permissible to sign off assessments carried out by another person.

12. Form 8 Part 3

We have seen that the first stage of completing Form 8 involves the SENCo (or the assessor working within the centre) gathering the centre-based evidence and detailing it within Part 1. This information is then used as the basis for the access arrangements assessment. The test results that are to be used as assessment evidence for access arrangements are then recorded by the assessor within Part 2, which is given to the SENCo.

The final part of the process is to complete Part 3.

$$1 + 2 = 3$$

It is the responsibility of the SENCo to make the final decision about which access arrangements a candidate has (where the access arrangement is centre-delegated) or applied for (for those that require approval). This decision is made after consideration of all the evidence that has been collated and recorded on Form 8: that which has come from the centre together with the assessment evidence.

In practice, the same person – the assessor working within the centre, or the SENCo who is qualified to carry out access arrangements assessments – may complete each section of Form 8.

Part 3 must be completed by the SENCo, or the assessor working within the centre, <u>after the candidate has been assessed</u>.

On the basis of Parts 1 and 2 of this form, record the access arrangements that will be applied for.

> The access arrangements that require approval are listed by the SENCo (or the assessor working within the centre) within Part 3.
> These could be:
> - 25% extra time
> - Scribe
> - More than 25% extra time (26% to 50% extra time)
> - Language modifier

Candidates may require several access arrangements, with different ones being used in different subjects or exams. For example, a candidate might use a scribe and 25% extra time in exams involving extended writing but prefer to write by hand in maths exams, only needing the 25% extra time.

Candidates may also need a computer reader or reader, which are not recorded on Form 8 but on a centre file note, or access arrangements that are centre delegated in addition to those requiring approval, such as the use of a coloured overlay and 25% extra time.

For JCQ purposes, there is no need to include details of the particular subjects or examinations that arrangements will be used in. There is also no requirement to include a computer reader or reader or any centre-based access arrangements in Part 3 of Form 8. However, this information will be needed for internal purposes so that arrangements can be facilitated. It is important, therefore, for the SENCo (or the ALS support team in FE) and the examinations officer to work together and devise a system that details the access arrangements (including centre-based arrangements), equipment (e.g. reading pen, bilingual dictionary) and paperwork (e.g. scribe cover sheet) the candidate needs for each examination.

The final part of Form 8 to be completed is the declaration.

Declaration

I am satisfied that the information provided on this form is accurate. I fully support the application and confirm that the candidate is/will be appropriately entered for the examination(s) concerned and will be able to demonstrate the assessment objectives required by the specification(s).

Candidate's name:	
Head of centre/SENCo or equivalent member or staff	
Name (Please print)	
Signature	
Date	

Either the Head of Centre, the SENCo, or an equivalent staff member signs to confirm that they are satisfied the information on the form is accurate, that they support the application for access arrangements and that the candidate has been entered for the appropriate examinations. It makes sense, therefore, for the declaration to be signed once the rest of the form is complete. It certainly needs to be done before any access arrangements are applied for.

The fully completed Form 8 is kept within the candidate's file in readiness for the JCQ Centre Inspection. The inspector may request to see the form, along with the accompanying evidence. This process is discussed in Chapter 16.

Part 3

The File Note
and Specialist Evidence

13. The Centre File Note

In Part Two of this Guide the requirements for Form 8 have been discussed in detail. Form 8 provides the access arrangements evidence for learners with cognition and learning needs who do not have an EHCP, IDP (in Wales) or SEN Statement (in Northern Ireland)[28]. We will now consider the route to access arrangements when an assessment does not take place.

Form 8 is not used for[29]:
- Communication and interaction needs
- Sensory and physical needs
- Social, emotional and mental health needs
- An EHCP, IDP (Wales) or Statement of Special Educational Needs (Northern Ireland) [30]
- Any candidate requiring a computer reader/reader

Although Form 8 and the associated assessment evidence is not required in these cases, both centre-based evidence and specialist evidence are needed for extra time or a scribe and there must written evidence for a reader/computer reader.

Centre-based evidence

The SENCo gathers the centre evidence in the same way as when compiling evidence for Form 8 Part 1. (See Chapter 6 for what is needed and methods of collecting the information.)

Once the required information has been compiled, the SENCo writes a file note to set out the centre evidence. This is a formal document and it needs to be written on centre-headed paper or on a template bearing the centre's logo. The finalised document is signed and dated by the SENCo (or equivalent staff member in FE).

The JCQ AARA document contains details of what needs to be covered in the file note. These are set out in bullet points within Chapter 5 of the AARA document, , as follows:

Access arrangement	AARA reference
25% extra time	5.2.3
26% to 50% extra time	5.3.2
Over 50% extra time	5.4.1
Computer reader/reader	5.5.5
Scribe	5.7.4

---

[28] Form 8 is required for 26% to 50% extra time for leaners with cognition and learning needs.
[29] Form 8 is required for a language modifier for all learners.
[30] This includes learners with cognition and learning needs requiring 25% extra time or a scribe.

For a **computer reader/reader**, the file note need only be short and concise, to confirm the nature of the candidate's impairment (i.e. briefly describe the reading difficulty) and that the use of a computer reader/reader reflects the candidate's normal way of working.

For the other arrangements, including **25% extra time**, the file note is more detailed and needs to:

- Confirm that the access arrangement is the candidate's normal way of working in the centre;
- Provide evidence from teaching staff that the candidate has persistent and significant difficulties, and how these substantially impact on teaching and learning.

For a **scribe**, the file note also needs to confirm that the candidate is not able to use a word processor without the spelling/grammar check/predictive text in every subject (hence the need for a scribe, rather than the candidate maintaining independence and using a word processor.)

For the two access arrangements involving more than 25% extra time, **26% to 50% extra time** and **more than 50% extra time**, further information needs to be added, including the maximum amount of extra time needed and how this has been determined. There also needs to be confirmation that:

- The difficulties have a very substantial impact on teaching and learning;
- The candidate is at a very substantial disadvantage when compared to other non-disabled candidates taking the examination;
- The extra time is the candidate's normal way of working as a direct consequence of his disability.

Examples of a file note templates for the following arrangements are provided on the next two pages:

- Computer reader/reader (and supervised rest breaks as a centre-delegated arrangement)
- 25% extra time and/or scribe

These are available for download from the Patoss website as a resource to accompany this Guide (see Appendix 2). The website resources also contain file note templates for:

- 26% to 50% extra time
- More than 50% extra time

You will need to copy the template onto centre-headed paper or add the centre logo to the template.

Centre File Note

Computer Reader/Reader or Supervised Rest Breaks

Candidate name: **Date of Birth:**   **Year Group:**

Indicate which access arrangement(s) the candidate requires:		

	✓ or X
Computer reader/reader *(AAO approval needed)*	
Supervised rest breaks *(Centre-delegated arrangement)*	

Confirm the nature of the candidate's impairment

Confirm that the arrangement is the candidate's **normal and current way of working within the centre.**

Form completed by: **Role:**

Signed: **Date:**

Centre Evidence for 25% extra time and/or scribe

Candidate name: **Date of Birth:**   **Year Group:**

Indicate which access arrangement(s) the candidate requires:

	✔ or X
25% extra time	
Scribe	

Confirm that the arrangement is the candidate's normal way of working in the centre.

Provide evidence from teaching staff that the candidate has persistent and significant difficulties, and how they substantially impact on teaching and learning.

For a candidate requiring a scribe, confirm that the candidate is not sufficiently competent or confident in using a word processor **with the spelling and grammar check or predictive text facility switched off** in every subject.

Form completed by: **Role:**

Signed: **Date:**

Patoss: This sheet can be photocopied without infringing copyright

Specialist evidence to accompany a file note

Just as Form 8 Part 2 must accompany Part 1, there must be specialist evidence to support the SENCo's file note (for extra time or a scribe). This can take a variety of forms and will depend upon the nature of individual candidate's difficulties.

The following are examples of evidence that can be used for this purpose:

Specialist Evidence	Notes
Education, Health and Care Plan (EHCP) IDP (in Wales) SEN Statement (Northern Ireland) [Note: Some EHCPs/IDPs/Statements contain highly confidential information relating to other family members, police protection, etc. It is important to be aware of confidentiality and data protection issues, both for storage and an application. Some Awarding Bodies will accept an extract of the EHCP that contains the relevant information or a redacted document.]	The EHCP (or IDP or Statement) confirms the candidate's difficulty or disability. It does not need to include assessment evidence or test scores that meet the JCQ assessment criteria. Neither does it need to make reference to, or recommendations for, access arrangements in tests or exams. The EHCP, IDP or Statement needs to be current (i.e. still in use) but it may have been issued earlier, such as in primary school or in early childhood. It will have been updated through Annual Reviews in secondary/further education.
Letter or report from CAMHS or an HCPC registered psychologist or a psychiatrist	For candidates with social, emotional and mental health needs and those with communication and interaction needs.
Letter or report from a medical consultant (GP evidence cannot be used)	For example, for a candidate who has a medical condition that could impact on performance in examinations (e.g. cerebral palsy, muscular dystrophy).
Letter or report from the Local Authority Educational Psychology Service	For a candidate who has undergone an assessment of their needs through a Local Authority EP. The assessment is likely to have taken place in the centre.

Letter or report from the Local Authority Sensory Impairment Service	For candidates with vision, hearing or other sensory needs. The letter will confirm the candidate's sensory disability.
Letter or report from the Occupational Health Service	For example, an Occupational Therapist specialising in Children and Young People Services, learning disability, or mental health.
Letter or report from a speech and language therapist (SaLT)	For candidates with speech, language and communication needs. The candidate will have undergone an assessment of their speech and language needs and may also have had support from a speech and language therapist.

The purpose of the specialist's evidence is to confirm the candidate's difficulty or disability; to provide verification that the difficulties are more than 'minor or trivial.' A note from a GP cannot be accepted for this purpose, the evidence must come from a specialist in the field of the difficulty as illustrated in the examples above.

The specialist's letter, report or documentation does not have to be written specifically for the purpose of providing evidence for access arrangements; in most cases, specialist evidence will already be in place as the difficulty is long term. The letter or report may have been written in the past and relate to the candidate at a younger age. For example, a learner with a hearing impairment may have had a series of investigations conducted, with letters from the Sensory Impairment Service summarising these investigations and their outcomes. As long as the information remains accurate, such that it reflects the candidate's current needs, it can be accepted as specialist evidence for access arrangements.

Equally, the specialist's letter, report or documentation is not expected to make recommendations for access arrangements in examinations. The specialist may not be (and in many cases is unlikely to be) familiar with the current JCQ regulations and the various access arrangements that are available to candidates. It would not be appropriate, therefore, for the specialist's evidence to stipulate the access arrangements that are needed.

The SENCo's file note, together with the evidence from the specialist, is kept in the candidate's file for inspection purposes.

Once both sets of evidence are in place (and the candidate has signed the Data Protection Notice), an application for access arrangements needs to be made through Access Arrangements Online.

In summary……

- When an assessment is not required, the SENCo or an equivalent member of staff writes a file note to set out the centre evidence.
- The file note must address each of the areas set out by the JCQ.
- Specialist evidence is needed to accompany the file note for extra time or a scribe.
- The evidence can be an EHCP, IDP or Statement, or a letter or report written by a specialist in the candidate's difficulty or disability.
- The evidence does not need to, and is not expected to, make reference to access arrangements.
- The specialist's evidence is stored along with the centre evidence and the signed data protection notice in the candidate's file.
- An application must be made online for those access arrangements requiring approval.

ASSESSING THE NEED FOR ACCESS ARRANGEMENTS DURING EXAMINATIONS – 6th EDITION

Part 4

Further Considerations

14. Applying for Access Arrangements On-line

In the previous chapters, the evidence requirements for access arrangements requiring approval from the JCQ or awarding bodies have been discussed in detail. Access Arrangements Online (AAO) is the system through which applications are made.

Access Arrangements Online is used to apply for access arrangements and to order modified papers for GCSE and GCE qualifications and a range of other Level 1, 2 and 3 qualifications. The JCQ AARA document specifies the qualifications that are covered by Access Arrangements Online.

Key facts:

- AAO enables centres to make a single online application for a candidate.
- It gives an instant response and the approval lasts for 26 months (see page 175 for further discussion of the '26-month rule').
- Applications for long-term conditions need to be made by specified deadlines.
- Over 90% of applications for access arrangements made through AAO are approved.
- Referrals to awarding bodies are also made through AAO.
- Appropriate documentation must be held on file for all applications for access arrangements made through AAO.
- AAO is also used for GCSE and GCE candidates who require access arrangements due to a temporary injury.

Pearson Access Arrangements Online (PAAO) Training Site

PAAO is set up in the same way as JCQ AAO and is used to process applications for Pearson Functional Skills and BTEC qualifications. However, access arrangements applications for Pearson GCSE and GCE are made through JCQ AAO.

A training site for Pearson Access Arrangements Online (PAAO) is available which enables you to make practice applications and check the questions that need to be answered before making 'live' applications.

As PAAO mirrors JCQ AAO, you can use the training site to practice JCQ AAO applications.

The training site is open access, so it is <u>vital</u> that no personal information that could identify an individual is used, as it will be visible to anyone using the site.

The PAAO training site is at **https://training.accessarrangements.pearson.com/** Click 'Exam centre log-in' to get started.

The AARA document contains a quick guide to using AAO. The following pages will explore making online applications and awarding body referrals for a range of candidates.

The data protection notice

Before making an online application for access arrangements, the candidate must provide his consent for his personal data to be processed and recorded online. This is achieved by the candidate signing the JCQ 'candidate personal data consent form.' Once completed, the form should be kept in the candidate's file for inspection purposes.

A candidate aged 13 years or over may sign the form. A parent is only required to sign the form where the candidate is unable to do so himself or to countersign the form where the centre deems it appropriate.

Each time a new online application is made, the candidate must sign a new data protection notice before the application is processed. This would apply when the candidate moves on from GCSE to GCE qualifications, if the candidate moves to a new centre, or if an additional access arrangement is added to the candidate's existing approved arrangements.

Who should make the AAO application?

Ideally, the SENCo or an equivalent member of staff will process the applications for access arrangements as she is the person who has collated all the paperwork and made the final decision on which access arrangements are to be applied for. The SENCo will, therefore, be best placed to answer the questions on the system.

It is not always possible, or practical, for the SENCo to complete the AAO applications - particularly in a large centre which may have hundreds (or even thousands) of applications! The Exams Officer often has a hand in processing the applications and it can work very well when both the SENCo and the Exams Officer work together to complete the applications.

Making an application

To get started, log in to an awarding body secure extranet site and go to the Centre Admin Portal (CAP).

The Centre Admin Portal (CAP) is the online system that is used for a range of examination related application and notifications. It allows centres to process alternative site arrangements, centre consortium arrangements, overnight supervision arrangements, transferred candidate arrangements and very late arrivals on-line. It also contains the JCQ interactive documents, including the AARA, and **Access Arrangements Online (AAO)**, through which centres process access arrangements applications and order modified papers.

> Before starting an application, check you have all the required documents evidencing the candidate's needs, both centre-based evidence and specialist/assessment evidence.

The AAO home page provides a series of options. To begin, select 'create access arrangements application'.

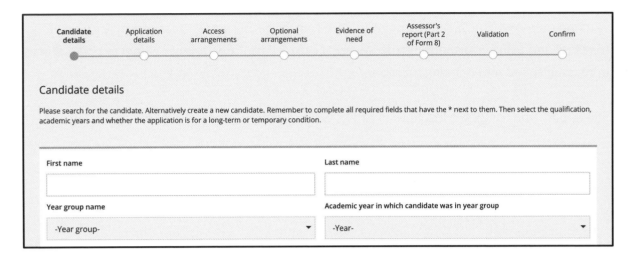

The top of the screen shows the various steps in making an application. The current step is shaded to indicate your progress. The first step is to enter the candidate onto the system.

Enter the candidate's details and click 'search'. If the candidate is not already on the system, the 'create candidate' tab will appear and you will be able to add the remaining details.

Next, select the qualification type, for example, GCSE, and whether the application is for a temporary condition (for which approval will last for one exam series) or a long-term condition (for which approval will be granted for 26 months). You also need to specify the academic year, or years, in which the access arrangements will be used.

Qualification type(s) *

☐ GCSE   ☐ GCE   ☐ Other

Application duration *

◯ Application for temporary condition   ◯ Application for long-term condition

Now select the access arrangements required for the candidate from the list (see next page). If the candidate requires more than one access arrangement, select each one.

> Make sure you have supporting evidence and can justify the need for each access arrangement otherwise the whole application will not be approved.

Examples

The following pages take you through example applications for three fictional candidates: Amy, Ben and Charlie.

Example A: 25% extra time for a learner with cognition and learning needs.

Amy is a learner who has a well-documented history of weaknesses in processing and working memory. The SENCo completed Part 1, after gathering feedback from Amy's teachers and using information from her ILP. Form 8 Part 2 documents below average scores in reading speed and working memory.

The application for 25% extra time in Amy's GCSE exams is processed as follows:

☐ Bilingual dictionary with 10% extra time (for the extensive use of the dictionary)

☐ Extra time over 25%

☐ Computer reader / reader

☐ Other

☑ 25% extra time

☐ Practical assistant

☐ Scribe/speech recognition technology

- We begin by selecting the access arrangement, 25% extra time, as shown above.

25% extra time

(5433) Does the candidate have learning difficulties in his/her first language which have a substantial and long term adverse effect on his/her speed of working? * ● Yes ○ No

(5434) Does the candidate have a long term physical disability which has a substantial and long term adverse effect on his/her speed of working? * ○ Yes ● No

(5435) Does the candidate have a medical condition which has a substantial and adverse effect on his/her speed of working? (The candidate's medical condition is not minor or trivial.) * ○ Yes ● No

(5436) Does the candidate have a sensory impairment, i.e. a visual impairment, a hearing impairment or a multi-sensory impairment, which has a substantial and long term adverse effect on his/her speed of working? * ○ Yes ● No

---

- The next screen (above) asks for the category of need. Only one question should be answered 'Yes', and the others should be answered 'No'.
  Quite often, a learner will have difficulties in more than one of these areas. However, for AAO, you need to select the primary area of need – that is, the one which your access arrangements evidence is based on.

- In Amy's case evidence gathered has shown learning difficulties which have a substantial impact on her speed of working so the first question (5433 above) would be marked 'Yes' with all the others marked 'No' as they are not relevant for her.

- The AAO system is interactive and different sets of questions will be generated based on the way the earlier questions are answered. Because we have specified that Amy has learning difficulties, the next screen will ask for evidence based on this category of need.

- For a candidate with learning difficulties, the evidence for 25% extra time can come either from specialist evidence in the form of an assessment (Form 8) or an EHCP, IDP or Statement. This is accompanied by the centre-based evidence, including the detailed picture of need (see Chapter 6).
  The questions on this screen relate directly to this evidence.

(5449) Has an assessment been completed, i.e. Part 2 of Form 8, to substantiate the picture of need, which is no earlier than the start of Year 9? *	⦿ Yes ◯ No

- Because Amy has been assessed and Form 8 has been completed, we can answer 'Yes' to the first question (5449 above).

(5450) Does a statement of special educational needs relating to secondary education exist, or an EHCP, to substantiate the picture of need? (The statement must confirm the candidate's disability.) *	◯ Yes ⦿ No

- Amy does not have a EHCP, IDP or Statement so we answer 'No' to the second question (5450 above).

> Note: If a candidate has an EHCP, IDP or Statement or but it has been decided, for some reason, not to use this as the basis for the access arrangements evidence and to use the 'Form 8 route' instead (i.e. to assess the candidate), you would select 'No' to the second question (5450 above) as the EHCP has not been used to support this application.

- Next, we are asked about the assessment evidence for 25% extra time. We select 'Yes' to confirm that Amy has two below average scores relating to two different areas of speed of working.

(5465) Has a detailed picture of need been painted which shows the JCQ Centre Inspector the requirement for 25% extra time as part of the candidate's normal way of working within the centre? *	Yes No

- We can also select 'Yes' for the final question (5465 above) as the SENCo has completed Form 8 Part 1 and has collated a detailed picture of need: Amy's ILP and questionnaires from teaching staff showing the need for extra time.

- On the next screen, a summary is shown of the questions that have been answered. It is important to check this carefully to make sure that you have answered each question correctly, based on the evidence you hold.

- At the bottom of the screen, you must confirm you have read and accepted the 'malpractice consequences statement,' after which you can submit the application.

The candidate must have signed a Data Protection Notice giving his/her consent to the processing of the application. You must have a signed Data Protection Notice at the time of processing the application.

Read and accept malpractice consequences statement

☑ Confirmation

On behalf of my centre I confirm that I have read and understand the terms of use of Access arrangements online and the JCQ regulations and guidance concerning access arrangements. To the best of my knowledge the information provided is accurate. Appropriate evidence to support the application is available within the centre for inspection.

- The following screen displays the outcome.
  In Amy's case, we have processed the application correctly and the evidence requirements have been met so the application can be approved instantly.

Application approved

This application will remain valid until the expiry date.

- The expiry date will be shown underneath the outcome, along with any exceptions (for example, 25% extra time - This access arrangement must not be used during exams testing the time in which a skill is performed, for example, sports, musical performance, expressive arts).

- The final step is the print out the approved application and place it in the candidate's file, where evidence is being stored in hard copy, or to save the approved application in the candidate's e-folder.

Example B – scribe with 25% extra time as an optional arrangement for a candidate with learning difficulties

Ben is a candidate who has substantial difficulties with spelling and writing. In the classroom, his writing is supported in different ways throughout the week, including the use of adaptations to his work, graphic organisers and spelling lists, support from a teaching assistant, and informal help with spelling from his friends.

For end of year exams, a teaching assistant acts as a scribe for Ben and, where possible, he has had this support in internal tests. When he uses a scribe, he needs to have his work read back constantly to keep track of his ideas and to make sure the scribe has recorded his dictation appropriately. At times, he needs to pause so that the scribe can catch up.

Ben will use a scribe for every exam and will require 25% extra time to use the scribe in all his exams. The SENCo has included this information within Form 8 Part 1 and Part 2 contains below average scores for writing speed and for spelling with unrecognisable attempts.

An application for a scribe with 25% extra time is made for Ben.

- On the first screen, the scribe/speech recognition technology option is selected.

When a scribe is applied for, there is the option of adding 25% extra time to the application (as noted in Chapter 4, on page 48).

The optional 25% extra time is tied in with the scribe. Form 8 Part 1 will specify why the extra time is needed with the scribe although separate assessment evidence is not required. In Ben's case, Part 1 might say, 'Ben needs time to organise his ideas and he needs to have his work read back constantly to keep track of his ideas and to make sure his dictation is recorded appropriately. At times, he needs to pause so that the scribe can catch up with his dictation. Ben will require 25% extra time alongside the use of a scribe in all his exams'.

Note: When 25% extra time is applied for in this way It cannot be used as a standalone arrangement. If the candidate will use 25% extra time without a scribe in any examination, this needs to be applied for separately with the relevant evidence in place.

- Having selected scribe/speech recognition technology, on the next screen you will clarify if you want the optional 25% extra time with the scribe. We select this option for Ben.

> **Select additional (optional) access arrangements**
>
> ☑ 25% extra time
>
> **Currently selected access arrangements**
>
> ☑ Scribe/speech recognition technology

- The next screen has a series of questions to answer

(5427) Does the candidate have a physical disability or a medical or psychological condition which has a substantial and long term adverse effect on his/her writing? *	◯ Yes ⦿ No
(5428) Does the candidate have a report from an assessor no earlier than the start of Year 9, i.e. Part 2 of Form 8, confirming substantial and long term writing difficulties in his/her first language? *	⦿ Yes ◯ No
(5429) Is the use of a scribe/speech recognition technology the candidate's normal way of working within the centre which is supported by clear evidence of need as per the JCQ regulations? *	⦿ Yes ◯ No
(5430) Does the candidate have a sensory impairment, i.e. a visual impairment, a hearing impairment or a multi-sensory impairment, which has a substantial and long term adverse effect on his/her writing? *	◯ Yes ⦿ No
(5431) Will the candidate be awarded 25% extra time on account of dictating to a scribe for the entire duration of the examination? *	⦿ Yes ◯ No
(5432) Does the candidate have an EHCP or statement of special educational needs relating to secondary education confirming substantial and long term writing difficulties in his/her first language? *	◯ Yes ⦿ No

In Ben's case, we would be answered 'Yes' to confirm the assessment evidence in Form 8 Part 2 (5428), that the use of a scribe is his normal way of working (5429) and that he will have 25% extra time to work with the scribe (5431).

- Now that we have confirmed that Ben has been assessed and there is a Form 8 Part 2 report, we are asked for the relevant scores from spelling and writing assessments.

- We need to specify
  - the assessor
  - the assessment date
  - whether the writing is illegible or grammatically incomprehensible
  - the spelling score and whether there are unrecognisable attempts
  - the writing speed score.

Only below average scores need to be included, as only below average scores provide assessment evidence for a scribe. In Ben's case, we give the below average scores for both spelling and writing speed.

- Ben's application is then submitted and approved.

- The approval includes details of exemptions and practical recommendations, including

25% extra time - This access arrangement must not be used during exams testing the time in which a skill is performed, for example sports, musical performance, expressive arts.

Scribe/speech recognition technology - This access arrangement must not be used for modern foreign language writing papers - unless the candidate spells out foreign words letter by letter, design papers except for writing, and ICT non-examination assessment.

Example C - Making an awarding body referral

Charlie is a candidate who has cerebral palsy. He has an extensive medical history, including a letter from a hospital consultant which confirms his physical disability. The SENCo has gathered centre-based evidence and written a file note. Charlie's normal way of working is to have 25% extra time and a practical assistant in exams and these arrangements will be applied for his GCSE examinations.

- An application for access arrangements is created for Charlie using AAO.

- 25% extra time and a practical assistant are selected.

- We confirm that Charlie has 'a long-term physical disability which has a substantial and long-term adverse effect on his speed of working.'

- Because a practical assistant is an access arrangement that cannot be granted by the online system, the application is not approved.

> Note: When an arrangement needs to be referred to an awarding body, none of the arrangements will be approved by the online system and the referral is made for all the access arrangements that are required by the candidate.

- We now have the option to make an awarding body referral. We start by clicking 'Send to awarding body.'

- Next, we select the awarding bodies that we need to send the referral to and provide the details of the specifications and the access arrangements we are applying for.

  In Charlie's case, we request 25% extra time and the practical assistant. We need to include precise details of the tasks that the practical assistant will perform so that the awarding bodies can decide whether the request is reasonable and appropriate and can ensure that the assessment objectives will not be compromised by the actions of the practical assistant.

- We then give details of the evidence for each of the arrangements.

- The referrals are then sent and we are issued with a receipt, which includes an application reference. The awarding bodies aim to respond to referrals within 10 working days. As our evidence is in order and our request is deemed reasonable and appropriate, the awarding bodies approve the application.

- We download and print the evidence cover sheet and store it in Charlie's file.

In summary...

- AAO is used to apply for access arrangements that require approval from the JCQ or awarding bodies.
- AAO covers a range of Level 1, 2 and 3 qualifications as specified in the AARA document.
- Before an application is made, you must ensure that you have all the required evidence to justify and support the access arrangements that are requested.
- Before an application is made, the candidate must sign a data protection notice to give his consent to his personal data being processed online.
- Applications for access arrangements due to long term conditions must be made by the published deadlines.
- The online system cannot approve 'high risk' or 'rare and exceptional' access arrangements. For these, a referral needs to be made to the awarding bodies.

15. Retaking and Moving On

In this chapter, we will look at the processes involved in maintaining access arrangements for a candidate with learning difficulties when approval expires. We will also discuss what happens when a candidate moves centres or from one level of study to another.

Retaking examinations at the same level

26 months

Let's begin by discussing what is sometimes known as the '26-month rule'. What is meant by this can differ depending on the particular access arrangements in place for a student.

The following table summarises the '26-month rule' for a candidate who continues to study at the same level in the same centre.

26-month rule		
Access arrangement	**Approval period**	**When approval expires**
• 25% extra time • Reader/computer reader* • Scribe	Approval is granted for 26 months from the date of the online application.	Reapply online using the existing evidence - no need to complete a new Form 8 or to reassess (for 25% ET, scribe).
• More than 25% extra time • Language modifier	Approval is granted for 26 months from the date that the assessment was carried out.	The process must start again – a new Form 8 and reassessment is needed.

Approval for 25% extra time, a reader/computer reader or a scribe

When the application is processed and approved, the approval lasts for 26 months from the date that the application is made online. For example, if the online application is made in the May of Year 9, the approval will last until the July of Year 11. The approval should, therefore, last for the whole of the candidate's GCSE study, unless retakes are needed.

Note: If an assessment is carried out early in Year 9, it can be worthwhile waiting until the May of Year 9 before making the online application so that the approval takes in the final exams in June of Year 11.

*Note: assessment evidence is not required for a reader/computer reader

Approval for 'rare and exceptional' access arrangements

The '26-month rule' is different for the rare and exceptional access arrangements, extra time over 25% and a language modifier. Both of these access arrangements require an application to be made through Access Arrangements Online. However, the online system cannot approve the arrangements and they will need to be referred to the Awarding Bodies for consideration (see Chapter 14).

If approval is granted by the Awarding Bodies, it lasts for 26 months from the date of the assessment, rather than the date of the application. For example, if a student is assessed in September of Year 9, the approval will last only until November of Year 11.

When approval runs out

If approval for 25% extra time, a computer reader/reader or a scribe expires, the centre can reapply for the access arrangements using the existing Form 8 (25% extra time, scribe) or file note (reader/computer reader), as long as the following conditions are met:

- The candidate continues to study at the same level (i.e. he continues to study GCSEs; he has not moved on from studying Level 2 to Level 3 qualifications).

  This situation might arise if an online application is made early in Year 9 and runs out before the final examinations in Year 11. It can also occur when a student retakes GCSE exams after Year 11.

- For 25% extra time, the detailed picture of need is updated (see Chapter 6)

- The candidate signs a new data protection notice, as a new application using the candidate's data is being processed online

- A new application is processed online, with approval granted for a further 26 months

For extra time over 25% and a language modifier, once the approval expires, it is not possible to reapply using the existing evidence even if the student is studying at the same level and within the same centre. In this situation, the whole process must begin again: the centre evidence must be gathered and recorded on a new Form 8 Part 1; the student must then be re-assessed and the new assessment evidence recorded in Form 8 Part 2; Part 3 and the Declaration must then be completed before a new application is made online.

Moving to another centre

If a candidate moves to another centre, there is an expectation that the SENCo will forward Form 8 and evidence of the assessor's qualification to the new centre. The existing Form 8 can continue to be used as evidence for 25% extra time or a scribe in GCSE examinations as long a series of checks is made to ensure that the evidence is complete and robust.[31]

The following checks must be made by the new centre:

- Has Part 1 of Form 8 been completed?

- Is there sufficient information within Part 1 showing the candidate's picture of need and normal way of working?

- Has Part 2 of Form 8 been completed?

- Are the tests recorded within Part 2 of Form 8 current, age appropriate and nationally standardised?

- Was the candidate assessed no earlier than the start of Year 9?

- Has Part 2 of Form 8 been signed and dated by the assessor?

- Has evidence been provided that the assessor holds, as a minimum, a post-graduate qualification in individual specialist assessment at or equivalent to Level 7? (i.e. a qualification certificate or a screenshot from the relevant website)

- Has Part 3 of Form 8 been completed?

- Has Part 3 of Form 8 been signed and dated by the SENCo?

If the checks are in order and the SENCo or Learning Support team are satisfied that the candidate continues to need the access arrangements, a new application is made through Access Arrangements Online, after the candidate has signed a new data protection notice. This will provide the approval for the candidate to continue to have the access arrangements in GCSE examinations (including resits) that are taken in the new centre.

Note: For **25% extra time**, an updated 'detailed picture of need' is required. This will involve the SENCo gathering centre-based evidence to support extra time in the new centre. This can be drawn from a sample of internal test or mock exam papers showing the application of extra time, an IEP or ILP referencing the need for extra time, or comments and observations of teaching staff as to why extra time is needed and how it is used.

---

[31] Information taken from *'Guidance regarding access arrangements/reasonable adjustments when a candidate changes centre'* available at https://www.jcq.org.uk/exams-office/access-arrangements-and-special-consideration/regulations-and-guidance

More than 25% extra time and a language modifier cannot be reapplied for using the existing evidence if a candidate moves to a new centre for GCSE retakes; the process must start again.

Moving on from GCSE to GCE study

Approval for access arrangements does not automatically pass from GCSE to GCE examinations. When a student progresses to A-levels, processes are in place to ensure that the access arrangements remain appropriate for the candidate at the new level of study. It is important to note that even if a student's approval for access arrangements has not expired, it cannot be carried forward and used for GCE exams; it becomes obsolete once the student has completed his GCSEs. This is the case even when the candidate remains in the same educational setting.

There are two possible routes that can be followed when a student moves onto GCE study, either to 'roll forward' the existing Form 8 or to start the process again and re-assess the candidate. The route to take depends on a number of factors, so let's look at each option in turn.

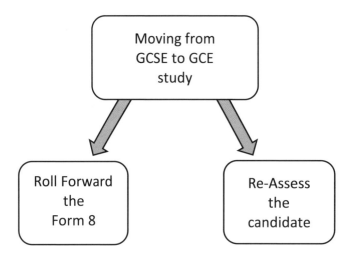

GCSE to GCE Roll Forward
The roll forward option can be used for the following access arrangements:
- 25% extra time
- Scribe

Form 8 can be rolled forward in the following situations:
- A student progresses from Year 11 into the Sixth Form of an 11 – 18 school.
- A student attends a new centre.

The rolling forward of a Form 8 from GCSE to GCE study is not an automatic process. The centre evidence must be updated, and a new application for access arrangements must be processed online.

Whilst the candidate does not need to be retested, there are a number of steps that need to be taken to roll forward a Form 8:

Step 1: Confirm the suitability of the existing Form 8

The questions in the table on page 177 will help when checking a Form 8. The SENCo must also ensure that the evidence contained within Part 2 of Form 8 meets the current published criteria for 25% extra time (i.e. there must two below average scores or one below average and one low average score relating to different areas of speed of working.)

Step 2: Update the centre evidence

Once a Form 8 is confirmed as being suitable to be rolled forward, the next step is for the SENCo to complete a file note to update the centre-evidence. This needs to be written on centre-headed paper and signed and dated by the SENCo.

To write the file note, evidence will need to be collected from teaching staff in the same way as is done when completing Form 8 Part 1. The file note needs to address two key areas as outlined in the JCQ regulations[32], as follows.

- Confirm that the access arrangement continues to be the candidate's normal way of working within the centre as a as a direct consequence of their disability within the meaning of the Equality Act 2010;
- Provide evidence from teaching staff that the candidate has p provide evidence from teaching staff that the candidate has persistent and significant difficulties, and how these substantially impact on teaching and learning.

File note templates for this roll forward process can be found in the downloadable resources that accompany this book (see Appendix 2).

Step 3: Attach file note as a cover sheet to the original Form 8

Once written, the file note is stapled to the front of the existing Form 8 and placed in the student's file for centre-inspection purposes.

---

[32] JCQ (2021) Access Arrangements and Reasonable Adjustments, 5.2.2 & 5.7.4, available at www.jcq.org.uk

> **Step 4: Have the student sign a new data protection notice**

The signed data protection notice provides the consent for the candidate's information to be processed online. The data protection notice is on the JCQ website.[33]

> **Step 5: Process an application online for GCE examinations**

The application for access arrangements (25% extra time and/or a scribe) at the new level of study then needs to be processed using Access Arrangements Online.

> **Step 6: Save the approval notice in the student's file**

The final step in the roll forward process is to save the approval sheet and store it in the student's file.

GCSE to GCE Reassessment

When a student moves on from GCSE to GCE study, the Form 8 cannot always be rolled forward. In the following situations, the roll forward process cannot be used:

- The student requires an access arrangement for which Form 8 cannot roll forward, i.e. extra time over 25%, language modifier;
- The original Form 8 paperwork is not sent on to the new centre;
- The original Form 8 paperwork is considered to be unsuitable to roll forward by the new centre (for example, there may be sections missing or incorrectly filled out);
- The assessment evidence for 25% extra time on the original Form 8 does not meet the current JCQ criteria;
- The new centre cannot obtain evidence of the original assessor's qualifications.

When Form 8 cannot be rolled forward, a reassessment needs to take place for the student's access arrangements to continue at the new level of study. The first step is for the SENCo to collect centre-based evidence and complete Form 8 Part 1. Sources of evidence will include feedback from teaching and support staff and may also include:

- Historical information about support in school;
- Details of former access arrangements;
- Information taken from the college admissions form, such as confirmation of a specific learning difficulty;

---

[33] The data protection notice is available at https://www.jcq.org.uk/exams-office/aao-access-arrangements-online/data-protection-notice

- Results from screening or initial assessments on entry to college;
- The student's self-reported difficulties and support strategies.

Once Part 1 is completed, the student is reassessed and the results recorded in Part 2, and then Part 3 is completed. The fully completed and signed Form 8 is placed in the student's file along with the signed data protection notice. For 25% extra time, the supplementary evidence for the detailed picture of need is also placed in the file.

The final step is to process a new application online for access arrangements at GCE level. The approval sheet should be printed off or saved electronically and placed in the student's file with the other documentation, ready for the centre inspection.

In summary...

Retaking qualifications at the same level
- For 25% extra time, a computer/reader, scribe - If approval for access arrangements expires and the candidate remains in the centre, reprocess an application using the same evidence.
- For 25% extra time or a scribe - If the candidate moves to a centre and the Form 8 is forwarded and found to be robust, reprocess an application using the same evidence. Update the detailed picture of need for 25% extra time.
- For 25% extra time or a scribe - If the candidate moves to a new centre and Form 8 and evidence of the assessor's qualification is not forwarded or not robust, start the process again.
- For extra time of more than 25% or a language modifier – if approval runs out or the candidate moves centre, start the process again.

Moving from GCSE to GCE study
- For 25% extra time or a scribe - If the candidate remains in the centre or moves to a new centre and the paperwork is on file/sent on and found to be robust,
  - Complete a file note to roll forward the Form 8,
  - Update the centre evidence for 25% extra time
  - Process an application for access arrangements in GCE exams.
- For 25% extra time or a scribe - If the candidate moves to a centre and the paperwork is not forwarded or not robust, start the process again.
- For extra time of more than 25% or a language modifier - if approval runs out, start the process again.

Note: Ensure the candidate signs a new data protection notice each time an AAO application is made.

ASSESSING THE NEED FOR ACCESS ARRANGEMENTS DURING EXAMINATIONS – 6th EDITION

16. The JCQ Centre Inspection

JCQ Centre Inspectors visit centres to scrutinise the documentation that supports approved applications for GCSE and GCE candidates. These visits often taken place during examination periods.

Storing paperwork

The SENCo is responsible for storing the access arrangements evidence for the JCQ Centre Inspection. The files need to be stored securely so that confidentiality is maintained.

Documentation can be stored either in hard copy (paper) format or electronically. If paperwork is stored in hard copy, the files will need to be kept in a locked filing cabinet. A separate folder is required for each candidate, with the paperwork organised in the same order in each one so that the contents can be checked easily.

If the SENCo decides to store the documentation electronically a secure e-folder needs to be created for each candidate. This must hold each of the required documents for inspection.

For each candidate, there must be a consistent method of storing documentation, with either all the evidence kept in hard copy or all held electronically.

In some cases, as a centre moves from storing hard copy documentation to electronic storage, different year groups within the centre may have evidence in different formats. This is perfectly fine, as long as each candidate's documentation is in a consistent format.

Note: Either hand-signed, electronic or typed signatures are acceptable for use on all access arrangements paperwork.

Whichever storage method is used, it can be helpful for the SENCo to create a checklist for each file, to ensure that the correct documentation is in place for each candidate. The next page contains an example of a checklist that could be used for this purpose. This is also available to download from the Patoss website (see Appendix 2).

Presenting the evidence

When the JCQ Inspector visits the centre, it is the SENCo who is expected to meet with the inspector and present the evidence. Sometimes, the SENCo may not be available at the time of the inspection visit. For example, the SENCo could work part-time, might be teaching a lesson, or could be absent from the centre for another reason. If the SENCo is not available, either the deputy SENCo or a member of the centre's senior leadership needs to meet with the inspector in place of the SENCo and address any queries that may be raised.

For this reason, it is important that preparations are made ahead of the centre inspection to ensure that the relevant member of staff understands the access arrangements systems and is able to present the paperwork and to answer questions during the Inspection visit.

> If the SENCo is unavailable, the Senior Leader (or deputy SENCo), not an Exams Officer, must meet with the inspector.

Access Arrangements: Checklist for candidates' files

	Tick when in file
Candidate name:	
Primary area of need for access arrangements:	
Access arrangements:	
Signed data protection notice	
Assessment evidence	
Form 8 Part 1 completed	
Form 8 Part 2 completed, signed & dated	
Part 3 and Declaration signed & dated	
Accompanying evidence for extra time (detailed picture of need)	
Non-assessment route	
File note completed, signed & dated	
Specialist evidence in place	
AAO Approval received and in file	

The inspector will generally ask to see the files for a selection of candidates from one or more year groups. Inspectors may focus on particular access arrangements within a centre, such as 25% extra time, or they could examine the paperwork for a selection of arrangements.

> Remember: The full supporting evidence must be in place before an application for access arrangements is processed through Access Arrangements Online.

Key issues

The table below sets out areas that the JCQ Centre Inspection Service has identified as issues during access arrangements visits.

Problem	Solution
Missing word processor policy	Ensure that the centre word processor policy is in place. 'A member of the centre's senior leadership team must produce a statement for inspection purposes which details the criteria the centre uses to award and allocate word processors for examinations[34].'
Missing evidence of the assessor's qualification(s)	Ensure evidence of the assessor's qualification(s) is in place before the assessment, e.g. print out from HCPC or SASC (or Patoss or Include-ed) website or copy of qualification certificate.
Incomplete Form 8: 1. Part 1 not completed, or 2. Part 2 is completed before Part 1	A picture of need and normal way of working is mandatory. Ensure that Form 8 Part 1 is completed and given to the assessor before the assessment takes place.
Incomplete Form 8: • Part 3 not completed	Ensure Part 3 is completed with the access arrangements that are to be applied for. The order of completion is Part 1, then Part 2, then Part 3.
Incomplete Form 8: • Part 2 not completed	1. Form 8 must contain the assessment evidence for access arrangements. Other methods of reporting test scores cannot be used. 2. If an assessment is not required, the SENCo must write a file note to set out the centre-based evidence. Form 8 Part 1 cannot be used for this purpose.
Scores within Form 8 Part 2 not in a standardised format	The assessor must report test scores as standard scores with a mean of 100. Other scoring systems, such as scaled scores (mean of 10), percentiles and words-per-minute scores cannot be used.

---

[34] JCQ (2021) Access Arrangements and Reasonable Adjustments, 5.8.4, available at www.jcq.org.uk

Incomplete Form 8: • Part 2 not signed by the assessor	Part 2 must be signed and dated at the same time the assessor records the test scores. It is not permitted for a member of centre staff to transfer scores from an external assessment report when the assessor has not provided Part 2. (e.g. a privately commissioned assessment conducted with no consultation with the centre.)
Incomplete Form 8: • Declaration not signed and/or dated	Ensure the Declaration is signed by either the SENCo (or equivalent staff member) or Head of Centre before the AAO application is made.
No centre-based evidence to accompany specialist evidence	Where specialist evidence such as an EHCP, a formal diagnosis of a medical or psychological condition or a sensory impairment is used, it must be accompanied by a file note written by the SENCo to set out the centre-based evidence.
Online processing error: Selecting all categories of impairment when processing an application	Select the candidate's principal impairment – the one which your evidence relates to.
No evidence to support a Form 8 rolling forward from GCSE to GCE qualifications	The centre-based evidence must be updated when a Form 8 rolls forward from GCSE to GCE. This applies for all candidates, including those who remain in the same centre.
No Data Protection Notice	Ensure that the candidate has signed the Data Protection Notice before the application is processed online. A new DPN must be signed by the candidate if a new application is processed.
No evidence available at the time of the inspection	Ensure that evidence is available when the JCQ Centre Inspector calls. A member of the senior leadership team must be briefed to present the evidence if the SENCo is not available.

If any problems are found, they will need to be rectified. Depending on the issues, a full scrutiny of the centre's files could take place, or a follow-up visit might happen to check that problems that were identified have been corrected.

Ensuring that the necessary paperwork is in place for all candidates requiring access arrangements that need approval means that the JCQ Centre Inspection will run smoothly.

17. Assistive Technology and Access Arrangements

There is a range of assistive technology that is available for candidates to use in examinations. As with any other access arrangement, the use of the equipment must be appropriate to the candidate's needs and reflect his normal way of working in the centre. The purpose of assistive technology is not to confer an advantage but enable access to the examination or assessment.

Benefits of using assistive technology

- Using technology can enable a candidate who requires support in examinations to work independently. This is a clear benefit as the learner is able to take control of his support requirements and does not have to rely on another individual for assistance. Promoting independent methods of working can help to build self-confidence. The ability to use assistive technology effectively is likely to have long-term benefits, including for older learners who will be either entering the workplace or moving on to higher education.
- The need for human support in the form of readers and scribes will be reduced in centres where assistive technology is used.
- Assistive technology for reading can be used in examinations in which reading is being tested, whereas a human reader cannot (N.B. extra time can be used in place of a reader in such circumstances).
- For young people, technology is an integral part of everyday life. A learner who may be resistant to support from a member of staff may be more open to using assistive technology as a method of support.
- Assistive technology may better reflect a learner's normal way of working in the classroom, particularly in centres where learning support assistants are not widely available.
  Where learning is taking place outside the centre (e.g. distance learning, home learning), assistive technology is more likely to reflect the normal way of working.

Considerations in using assistive technology

- Cost can be a major factor in a centre providing assistive technology. Some equipment can be expensive to purchase and maintain, although this needs to be balanced against the costs involved in providing human support.
- Candidates must have ample practice and training in using equipment and be confident using it.
- There are several programs that provide support for reading and writing. It can take time to find the software that works best for the learners in your setting, and this

may vary from one learner to another. The choice can seem daunting, and time and a degree of expertise are needed to find the best solution for each learner.

- Assistive technology will not be appropriate for all learners. Some will not be able to use the equipment and will need support in the form of a reader or scribe.

Examples of assistive technology

Examination Reading Pen

An exam reading pen is a portable device that is used for reading single words or short pieces of text. The candidate scans the text, which is displayed on the device and spoken aloud. Earphones are supplied with the exam reading pen so that the candidate can be situated in the main exam hall without disturbing others.

The use of an exam reading pen is a centre-delegated access arrangement. It should reflect the candidate's normal way of working although no formal evidence is required for its use.

A benefit of the exam reading pen is that it can be used in papers that are testing reading.

Note: If an exam reading pen is used in place of a human reader in an exam testing reading, the candidate cannot have up to 50% extra time in place of the reader.

In the classroom, a reading pen with additional functions can be used. It includes a built-in dictionary, and text can be either recorded and saved to the device or saved directly to a computer so that it can be played back later. Whilst this version cannot be used in exams, it can be a helpful device to support reading during study.

Word processor

The use of a word processor is a centre-delegated access arrangement as long as spell-check, grammar-check and predictive text functions are switched off. Either a computer or a tablet can be used for this arrangement.

Whilst the use of a word processor does not need to be applied for, each centre must have a policy on the use of word processors that is shared with students and parents. In addition, a member of the centre's senior leadership team must produce a statement setting out the criteria that are used to allocate word processors for examinations.

This arrangement can be useful in the following situations:

- A candidate whose handwriting is illegible or extremely slow.

- A candidate who has difficulties with planning and organisation when writing by hand, and for whom the quality of writing can improve significantly when using a word processor.
- A candidate in a centre where much of the curriculum is delivered through the use of IT and where using a word processor is the normal method of writing for all learners.

Word processor with spell-check, grammar-check (and predictive text) enabled

For a candidate who has an approved application for a scribe, there is the option of using a word processor with spell-check, grammar-check and, where needed, predictive text facilities enabled. Using a word processor in this way in place of a scribe can promote the candidate's independence.

It should be noted that, just as when a scribe is used, the candidate will not have access to marks awarded for spelling, punctuation and grammar (SPaG) unless these are done independently.

When a word processor is used as a scribe option in this way, a scribe cover sheet (and not a word processor cover sheet) must be submitted.

Speech recognition technology (speech-to-text software)

Speech recognition software is another option for candidates who have an approved application for a scribe. As with the use of a word processor, this option can give the learner independence.

The candidate dictates into a computer and, just as when a scribe is used, the dictated responses can be read back to the candidate so that they can be checked for accuracy. The optional arrangement of 25% extra time to accompany a scribe will be useful in providing time for the candidate to check that the transcription of the dictation is accurate.

Again, the candidate will not have access to marks awarded for spelling, punctuation and grammar (SPaG) unless these are done independently.

Computer reader (Text-to-speech software)

A computer reader, or text-to-speech software, requires permission to be used in exams. It has the same criteria as a reader (i.e. a file note written by the SENCo) and the two arrangements are applied for together using Access Arrangements Online so that the centre, together with the candidate, can decide which option is used in each exam. A computer reader can be used in papers that are testing reading, whereas a reader cannot. (Note: Up to 50% extra time can be used in place of a reader in sections of papers testing reading when a computer reader is not used and the candidate reads independently.)

Some candidates can find it challenging or embarrassing to ask a reader for text to be read, especially when they require the same piece of text to be read more than once. Because candidates work independently with a computer reader, and do not need to ask for help, the use of a computer reader may give them more confidence to listen to text being read as many times as they need.

If a candidate uses a word processor for writing along with a computer reader, his own work can also be read back and checked for clarity and accuracy.

To use a computer reader, the centre will need to upload the exam paper to the computer. This can be achieved either by:

- Ordering a non-interactive PDF question paper.
- Opening the question paper packet early under secure conditions to scan the question paper.

In summary...

- There is a range of assistive technology available to candidates who require access arrangements in exams.
- Some options require approval whilst others are centre-delegated.
- Any arrangement must reflect the candidate's normal way of working and it is vital that the candidate has had ample time to practice using the equipment and is fully confident in doing so.

---

18. Access Arrangements for Students with English as an Additional Language (EAL)

by Caroline Read & Gurinder Grewal

For the purposes of this chapter when considering the needs of a candidate with EAL, there is an expectation by the JCQ and awarding bodies that the level of English is sufficient to take part in the UK exam system, *'The centre must assess each potential learner and make justifiable and professional judgements about the learner's potential to successfully complete and achieve the qualifications.'*[35] In some cases, the candidate would be better advised to delay their attempt to gain qualifications until they have acquired a better knowledge of the English language.

The JCQ 'Access Arrangements and Reasonable Adjustments' (AARA) offers two access arrangements specifically intended for candidates with English as an additional language:

- Bilingual dictionary
- Up to 10% extra time to use the dictionary, in some circumstances.

Bilingual dictionary

Where the first language is not English, Irish or Welsh and the use of a bilingual dictionary is the normal way of working, the candidate may use a dictionary in most exams and assessments. The dictionary may take the form of either an electronic or hard copy dictionary. No monolingual dictionaries are allowed, nor are translators (including online translators), wordlists or glossaries. Whatever format the dictionary takes it should include word for word translations, with no clarification or pictures. A concise dictionary would be appropriate. The dictionary must be kept in the centre for the exam series and should be checked for unauthorised notes and revision data at the start of the series. Ideally, a second copy of the student's preferred dictionary would be kept in the exams office.

There are some subjects in which dictionaries are not permitted. Examples include; English, Irish or Welsh, and subjects assessing spelling, punctuation and grammar (SPaG) (English literature, geography, history and religious studies). For modern foreign languages candidates may not have access to a dictionary in the language being assessed so, e.g., there can be no French/English dictionaries in a French assessment. The same is the case if languages are similar so, e.g., no Portuguese dictionary would be permitted in a Spanish exam. There are a few exceptions to this rule where the appropriate dictionary **can** be used. These are the Writing Tests in GCSE Bengali, GCSE Modern Hebrew and GCSE Panjabi where the specification states that all candidates must have access to a bilingual dictionary.

Under no circumstances is it permitted to translate a paper or responses to or from the first language.

---

[35] JCQ (2021) Access Arrangements and Reasonable Adjustments, 3.1, available at www.jcq.org.uk

Bilingual dictionary with 10% extra time

For Level 2 qualifications (e.g. GCSE) but not Level 3 (GCE), in rare and exceptional circumstances, up to a maximum of 10% extra time may be granted to use the bilingual dictionary. An application should be made through Access Arrangements Online (AAO) if each of the following conditions has been met. The candidate:

- has been in the UK for less than three years (including holidays)
- came with no prior knowledge of English
- was not taught in English or prepared for qualifications using English prior to UK arrival
- English is not spoken at home
- needs to use the dictionary extensively, delaying the answering of questions
- extra time to use the dictionary is the normal way of working

Other arrangements which can be granted by the centre

As well as these two arrangements for candidates with EAL, there are a few arrangements which can be granted for any candidate (without an application through AAO) because they are the candidate's 'normal way of working' in the classroom. Some of these might apply to a candidate with EAL, e.g.

- Supervised rest breaks (appropriate evidence needed on file)
- Word processor (spelling and grammar check switched off)
- Read aloud
- Exam reading pen
- Prompter
- Coloured paper/overlays

Arrangements requiring an application through AAO

Other commonly used arrangements, such as readers, scribes and extra time, can only be granted if the candidate has a learning difficulty, or another substantial impairment, such as a physical disability or sensory impairment.

In the case of candidates with a substantial impairment or disability confirmed by documentation from a suitable source (e.g. a psychologist, psychiatrist, hospital consultant, teacher of the visually or hearing impaired, speech and language therapist, or an EHCP, IDP or SEN Statement) this is fairly straightforward. The candidate may have access to the appropriate arrangement as long as a file note is provided by the centre showing that the arrangement is used and needed in class, and an application approved through AAO (see Chapter 13 on the use of file notes).

In relation to applications for candidates with learning difficulties Access Arrangements Online requires the centre to answer the following questions:

Reader: Does the candidate have substantial and long-term reading and/or comprehension difficulties in his first language?
Scribe: Does the candidate have learning difficulties in his first language which have a substantial and long-term adverse effect on his writing?
Extra Time: Does the candidate have learning difficulties in his first language which have a substantial and long-term adverse effect on his speed of processing?

JCQ Form 8 Part 1 states: If the candidate's first language is not English, you must show that he has underlying difficulties in his first language. The candidate's difficulties must not be due to their limited acquisition of the English language. Please record this information under Part 1 – 'Any other relevant information'.

These statements are often interpreted to mean that assessors must conduct an assessment in the candidate's first language. However, this cannot be the case as there are very few psychometric assessments available in languages other than English, and even where they exist, finding a qualified assessor to carry out those assessments will present a challenge. On occasion, a candidate may have been assessed previously and have a report written in a foreign language. Where possible, such a report should be translated as it can provide clear evidence of the existence of a learning difficulty. This information should be summarised in the 'Any other relevant information' box in Part 1 of Form 8. However, such cases are few and far between. So, in most cases, we have to establish whether the EAL candidate has an underlying difficulty using tools in the medium of English.

Establishing underlying learning difficulties in EAL students

Learning Difficulty or Language Difficulty
"Difficulties related solely to limitations in English as an additional language are not SEN."
SEND Code of Practice [36]

With the majority of EAL learners, lack of fluency in English would usually be perceived as a language barrier to learning as opposed to a special educational need in cognition and learning. These learners will need sufficient learning opportunities to develop their English language skills before a decision can be made about the possible presence of a learning difficulty. Therefore, we cannot assume that every EAL candidate can have access arrangements based on evidence of weak literacy skills or slow speed of processing.

We also know that some learners are mistakenly thought to have special educational needs when they are going through the normal second language acquisition stages for bilingual learners. Conversely, some EAL learners may not be identified as having SEN because their lack of progress is attributed to difficulties learning English as an additional language.

---

[36] Department for Education (2015) Special Educational Needs and Disability Code of Practice: 0 to 25 years

Because of their varying educational experiences, EAL learners vary greatly in what they can say or write, and what they know or can understand. Some have better developed literacy skills and less well-developed verbal skills, and vice versa. These discrepancies should not be used to identify a learning difficulty. When EAL learners start school, there is often a silent period which may last several months. During this period, they are actively listening but not expected to speak. This behaviour is normal and should not be misinterpreted as the learner having a learning difficulty.

The errors that second language learners make with spelling, writing, grammar, punctuation, and reading comprehension in the natural process of language acquisition are similar to those produced by native speakers with learning difficulties. EAL learners may confuse sounds, transpose letters in words, have poor handwriting and sentences may not make sense. Short term memory difficulties and slow speed of processing can also manifest when the EAL learner feels overloaded, struggles to grasp concepts and is still thinking in their first language, often resulting in having to translate meaning from one language to the other.

It is clear then that providing evidence of a learning difficulty in EAL learners for the purposes of access arrangements is not straightforward.

Issues with assessments for learning difficulties
Carrying out assessments in the learner's first language would be the first consideration. However, the lack of validated reliable screening tools and scientific testing instruments available in other languages, together with a shortage of qualified specialists to administer them make this an unrealistic option.

Translating materials from English into the target language is not recommended because of some of the inappropriateness or irrelevance of the cultural and linguistic items within the English tools.

Carrying out assessments in the English language is the only remaining option, but the following limitations need to be observed: tests have not been standardised on the EAL population; they often have a cultural/ linguistic bias; and they do not give accurate info about the learner's abilities.

'Assessment in this area requires normal good assessment practice as well as an extra emphasis on knowledge and understanding of how a first language(s) (L1) might affect performance in tests of literacy attainment and cognitive processing in a second language (L2) i.e. English.'[37]

---

[37] SpLD Assessment Standards Committee (SASC) (2019), Guidance on the assessment of individuals for whom English is an additional language (EAL) and/or where there is a complex linguistic history, available at: www.sasc.org.uk

A key element of normal good assessment practice is the gathering of high-quality background information which enables us to contextualise the assessment data and eliminate as many other possible causes for the difficulties presented. The latter is especially important in the case of EAL learners, a heterogeneous population. Specific factors to consider include:

- The learner's level of language proficiency: the learner's level of English may not be at the level required to meet the demands of the curriculum. Measurements of attainment may be misleading if assessments are carried out before English proficiency is reached.
- The extent to which the learning environment is supportive: the learner needs to feel settled, safe and valued in an inclusive environment.
- The extent to which the learner has access to the curriculum: the learner needs to receive adequate EAL support to ensure that he/she is able to access the curriculum effectively.

Additionally, the possibility of the following should be considered:

- Cultural differences which may result in them being reserved and withdrawn at school or unable to relate to others around them; or being unfamiliar with particular customs and traditions, thus feeling excluded. There may also be a stigma associated with learning difficulties in particular cultures, possibly resulting in difficulties being masked or ignored.
- Trauma experienced in the past, affecting wellbeing, and making it difficult to pay attention and sustain concentration.
- Unstable home life, perhaps having had to move house several times, which is unsettling and not conducive to learning.
- Undisclosed health issues could be affecting their learning

Importance of gathering information about the EAL learner's functi0oning in their first language and their current functioning in English

EAL learners' overall level of proficiency in their second language is affected by: the orthography, complexity and level of transparency of their first language; the extent to which they are literate in their first language; and how proficient they are in speaking both their first language and the second language. It is known that strengths and weaknesses in the first language transfer to the development of the second language.

When attempting to address the source of an EAL candidate's difficulties we need to know the student's starting point. For example, if a student started in Year 8, had no English knowledge prior to this, and their first language had a different script, how quickly could we expect them to have secure sound-symbol correspondence or write at an average speed and spell accurately? Some skills, which are usually learnt at primary school by first language English students, are never learnt formally by some EAL learners so the 'foundations' of the language are not there.

Addressing the challenges

This brings us back to ensuring that centres gain reliable background information on the candidate to help establish whether a learning difficulty does exist. All the information collated from various sources is vital. *'The assessment and identification process is multi-disciplined and requires information from many sources in order to make a correct identification.'* [38] This evidence would be noted in Part 1 of Form 8 and may include the following:

- Results from a screening questionnaire, which ask questions concerning typical behaviours relating to different types of learning difficulties
- Background information/educational history indicating difficulties with acquiring and developing literacy or language skills and any support provided
- Observations from teaching and support staff, etc. which point to the existence of a learning difficulty and details of any adjustments and support provided
- The student's own comments/observations and, where appropriate, information from parents
- Qualitative information gained from informal testing
- Summary of any previous assessment carried out in the native language

The outcome of screening questionnaires, which ask questions concerning typical behaviours relating to different types of learning difficulties will be crucial here. Most assessors will have such tools in their assessment materials.

In some cases, limited acquisition of English may, in itself, be evidence of a learning difficulty, especially if the candidate came to the UK in Key Stage 1 or early Key Stage 2. Many primary teachers will testify to seeing non-English speakers arriving at school in September, who demonstrate a functional level of 'playground' English by the end of the autumn term. Candidates who are still struggling to acquire a functional level of English by Year 9 or 10 may well have learning difficulties.

The following types of assessment and approaches have been used to gather information concerning the needs of EAL candidates. It is important to watch closely how the candidate responds to each test and ask them about the strategies they are employing.

Working Memory
- Digits (and possible, letters) forwards and backwards
- Visual memory

Rapid Naming
- Ask the candidate to name in English

---

[38] Haldimann, M. and Hollington, A. (2004) *Effective Learning Support in International Schools.* John Catt Educational Ltd.

- Then ask them to name in the first language
- It will be necessary to work out how many syllables the numbers/letters used in the English version of the test and the numbers in the version conducted in the first language contain, as this will affect the time needed to say the numbers.

The results in the first language **cannot** be reported as standard scores, and of course, it won't be possible to check the accuracy of naming in the candidate's first language, but qualitative analysis may help to establish whether processing issues are due to English vocabulary difficulties or processing speed difficulties.

Visual Information Processing and Visual Motor Integration
- For example, Beery Buktenica VMI, Symbol Digit Modalities Test, DASH Graphic Speed

Assessors should be mindful of the cultural impact of previous learning here, for example, did drawing feature in the candidate's previous education?

Reading
- If possible, compare reading speed in English and first language, though it will not be possible to be sure that the texts compared carry the same level of complexity.
- Reading comprehension measures can be less reliable - beware of low scores as a result of EAL

Writing speed and handwriting
- Assess legibility (legibility may be more of an issue for a candidate whose first language does not use a Roman script)
- Free writing speed as measured by the Detailed Assessment of Speed of Handwriting, suggested adaptations:
  - Ask for two pieces of writing:
    - one in English
    - one in own language
  - The comparison **may** help to establish whether speed is:
    - a language issue
    - a writing speed issue

Assessors must keep in mind that EAL candidates may not have carried out much writing in their first language. However, if they write little in English but fluently in their first language, it is fair to assume that their difficulty is due to limited English language acquisition.

Assessors must remember that many students 'lose' their first language literacy skills within a short period of time if they are not practised as they did not reach any level of proficiency in those skills. This should be considered when making comparisons between English and first language.

In summary...

The existence of an underlying learning difficulty will be based on persistent problems with the acquisition and development of literacy skills, and lack of progress in learning compared with the level the student was at when they came to the UK.

Of course, as we noted earlier, other causes for those difficulties may need to be considered, for example, psychological issues such as trauma, social issues: settling in, moving around, and health related conditions.

Where a candidate is thought to need access arrangements because of an underlying learning difficulty, centre-based evidence, which includes details of a history of difficulties in the learner's native language, will need to be obtained and the assessor will need to carry out appropriate testing of literacy and processing skills to meet the JCQ assessment evidence criteria, just as they would for a native English speaker.

19. Other Qualifications

In this chapter, access arrangements in qualifications other than GCSE and GCE will be discussed.

Qualifications covered by the JCQ

General qualifications

A variety of general qualifications are studied by learners in secondary and further education. These are at Entry Level and Levels 1, 2 and 3 of the National Qualifications Framework.

Access Arrangements Online is used to process access arrangements requiring approval in the following qualifications:

- AQA Applied General qualifications
- AQA Level 1, 2 and 3 Technical qualifications
- Cambridge Nationals and Cambridge Technicals
- FSMQ
- GCSE and GCE
- OCR Level 3 Certificates
- Welsh Baccalaureate Qualification (WBQ)
- WJEC Level 1 and Level 2 General qualifications
- WJEC Level 1 and Level 2 Vocational qualifications
- WJEC Level 3 Applied qualifications

Entry Level Certificate qualifications

AAO is not used for Entry Level Certificate (ELC) qualifications. Many access arrangements are centre-delegated and do not need to be recorded. Form 11 must be completed online through the Centre Admin Portal (CAP) for candidates who require:

- Bilingual dictionary with 10% extra time (for the use of the dictionary)
- Computer reader/reader
- Extra time in timed components
- Practical assistant
- Scribe

Assessment evidence is not required. The SENCo or equivalent staff member must determine the need for the arrangement based on normal classroom practice.

Where a reader, scribe, communication professional or practical assistant is used, Form 13 must be downloaded from the Centre Admin Portal (CAP) and placed inside the candidate's script.

ELC – Reader/Computer Reader:
In ELC English, a reader is not permitted in the Reading component. A computer reader may be used where it is the candidate's normal way of working within the centre.

A candidate who would normally be eligible for a reader, but is not permitted this arrangement, can have up to 50% extra time to read independently.

ELC – Communication Professional using Sign Language:
Communication Professionals cannot not be used in English, Irish and Welsh Speaking and Listening Tests and in English, Irish and Welsh written papers, except for the instructions of the question papers, unless specifically permitted by the specification at certain levels.

In English, Irish and Welsh reading tests no part of an assessment may be signed to a candidate. However, the candidate may indicate using sign language to show that he or she has read the passage correctly.

Vocational qualifications
Chapter 2 of the JCQ AARA document contains information about vocational qualifications. Awarding bodies have a duty to make reasonable adjustments where an assessment arrangement would put a disabled person at a disadvantage in comparison to a non-disabled person. Many of the access arrangements listed within the AARA document will be available to candidates taking vocational qualifications. However, there are exceptions where competence standards would be invalidated if an adjustment was to be made, and advice may need to be sought from the awarding body. Any reasonable adjustment must reflect the normal learning or working practice of a learner in a centre or workplace.

Form VQ/IA is used to record reasonable adjustments in internal assessments. This is held on file in the centre.

Form VQ/EA is used for reasonable adjustments in externally assessed units and is sent to the awarding body at least 6 weeks before the date of the assessment series. VQ/EA is also used to apply for modified papers.

Qualifications not covered by the JCQ

Access arrangements, evidence requirements and application processes vary and can change each year. Contact the relevant awarding body for advice in relation to each qualification.

Functional Skills
The JCQ regulations (the AARA document) do not cover Functional Skills qualifications. Awarding bodies publish their own guidance on access arrangements and advice must be sought from the relevant awarding body in relation to access arrangements and evidence requirements for candidates taking Functional Skills qualifications.

BTEC and IGCSE (Pearson/Edexcel)

Contact Pearson/Edexcel for guidance.[39]

Cambridge International Examinations (CIE) IGCSE

Documentation is available on the CIE website.[40] The Cambridge Handbook and the leaflet, 'Good practice guide: Running exams involving access arrangements and candidates with disabilities' are useful sources of information.

Access arrangements in end of Key Stage National Curriculum tests (SATs)

Guidance on access arrangements is available from the gov.uk website.[41] Access arrangements are based primarily on normal classroom practice and are available for learners who have, for example, difficulties in reading, writing, processing and concentrating, as well as those with a hearing or visual impairment.

Access arrangements in higher education

Students who require support in higher education, including access arrangements in examinations, are required to provide evidence confirming a disability in line with the Equality Act 2010. This will be either medical evidence or, for learners with a specific learning difficulty, a report from a diagnostic assessment which confirms a specific learning difficulty, such as dyslexia. The assessment needs to have been carried out by a qualified specialist teacher holding a current SpLD Assessment Practising Certificate or by an HCPC registered psychologist. Form 8 is unlikely to be sufficient evidence for access arrangements.

Students with a learning difficulty, health problem or disability entering higher education can apply for Disabled Students Allowance (DSA), which can help with the costs of specialist study support, specialist equipment and other disability-related costs.[42]

The Disability Service of the university will be able to provide information on support and access arrangements in higher education.

In summary…

- AAO is used to apply for access arrangements in a range of Level 1, 2 and 3 qualifications from JCQ awarding bodies.
- Where AAO is not used, contact the relevant awarding bodies or organisations for information and advice on access arrangements.
- Arrangements in national curriculum tests are based on normal classroom practice.
- Access arrangements in higher education usually require evidence from a diagnostic assessment or relevant medical evidence.

---

[39] Contact details for Pearson/Edexcel can be found at http://qualifications.pearson.com

[40] Documentation relating to access arrangements in Cambridge International Examinations can be found at www.cambridgeinternational.org

[41] Key Stage 2 access arrangements guidance, available at https://www.gov.uk/government/publications/key-stage-2-tests-access-arrangements

[42] Information on DSA available at https://www.gov.uk/disabled-students-allowances-dsas

20. Frequently Asked Questions

These questions are drawn from those most commonly received through the Patoss Helpline and at training events. They are listed under themes. In all cases, further information can be found in earlier chapters of this Guide and in the JCQ regulations.

Extra Time

1. What is a 'detailed picture of need' when a learner requires 25% extra time?

See Chapter 6 for discussion. In summary, a detailed picture of need is supplementary centre-based evidence showing the need for extra time for a candidate with learning difficulties. This evidence can be drawn from the following sources: a sample of internal school tests or mock exam papers showing the application of extra time (e.g. the learner changes pen colour to show how extra time is used), an IEP/ILP referring to the need for extra time, or comments and observations from teaching staff as to why the candidate needs extra time and how this is used. The documentation is summarised in Form 8 Part 1 and kept in the candidate's file for JCQ Centre Inspection purposes.

2. What is the best test for extra time?

It depends! A selection of useful cognitive processing tests is listed in Chapter 10, along with measures of reading speed and writing speed. Two or more scores are needed in different areas relating to speed of working. There is no single test that will be useful in providing the evidence for all learners requiring extra time, as areas of strength and difficulty vary from one individual to another. For these reasons, a range of tests is required, and more than one test will be needed to establish the assessment evidence required.

3. When can I use only low average scores for extra time?

In the vast majority of cases, learners with cognition and learning needs (i.e. those for whom assessment evidence is required) will have at least one below average score and one low average score relating to different areas of speed of working. Others will have two below average scores. These are the standard expected categories providing the assessment evidence for 25% extra time. It is possible to use low average scores when there is a substantial weight of centre-based evidence that shows the need for 25% extra time. However, one low average score by itself is not sufficient. There must be at least two relating to two different areas of speed of working.

The use of low average scores should be considered an exception and the application will not be approved through AAO; it will need to be referred to the relevant awarding bodies. The centre would have to provide a clear and detailed justification for the extra time.

4. A candidate in our centre requires 25% extra time. I have assessment evidence showing two low average scores using relevant tests. Why was my application rejected by Access Arrangements Online?

See Question 3 above. Only 'standard' applications for access arrangements can be approved through AAO. When a request for 25% extra time is made with no below average scores relating to speed of working, the application will not be approved by AAO. A referral must be made to the awarding bodies, who will examine the evidence provided and make a decision on whether to approve the application.

5. Can two subtest scores from the same composite be used as 'two different areas relating to speed of working'?

No. Two subtests that contribute to the same composite cannot be used as 'two different areas of speed of working.' They are considered to measure the same skill, domain or area of processing. Two different areas would be either:

- Speed of reading and speed of writing
- Speed of reading and cognitive processing
- Speed of writing and cognitive processing
- Two different areas of cognitive processing

For 'two different areas of cognitive processing', scores must come from two tests that measure different skills or different types of processing, or from two subtests contributing to different composites. For example, working memory and phonological awareness; visual processing and phonological memory; rapid naming (phonological processing speed) and phonological memory. See JCQ AARA 7.5.12 for examples of areas of processing.

6. Can I give extra time or rest breaks for exam stress?

No. It is not unusual for candidates to be nervous about sitting public exams, particularly when their next steps in education are reliant on achieving particular grades. You should teach exam management strategies.

A distinction needs to be made between those candidates who feel nervous about exams and those who have genuine mental health needs for which they are undergoing investigation or treatment from a specialist. Where there is a substantial difficulty supervised rest breaks, or in some cases, 25% extra time may be appropriate provided that the relevant evidence is in place.

7. Where does the school stand in regard to privately commissioned reports from psychologists or specialist teachers that recommend extra time?

The Head of Centre decides whether to accept or reject the recommendations of the report in relation to access arrangements. Any rejection would not be based on a dispute over the diagnosis made by the professional but on the system not having been followed correctly.

Private assessors must make contact with the centre to obtain Part 1 and provide evidence of their qualifications before the assessment is conducted. Following the assessment, test scores that are to be used as assessment evidence must be provided on Form 8 Part 2. Failure to comply with these regulations means that a privately commissioned assessment cannot be used as evidence for access arrangements.

If the private assessor follows the correct procedures, the evidence may be accepted.

We recommend open and early communication with candidates (and their parents where appropriate) to encourage joint working with the centre to help to avoid such situations.

8. Can a student have 25% extra time as well as a reader and/or a scribe?

25% extra time in addition to a reader and/or a scribe is not an automatic right. If the 25% extra time is to be used alongside a scribe (and not as a standalone arrangement), Form 8 Part 1 needs to include details of why the candidate needs extra time when using a scribe. Separate assessment evidence is not needed. When the application is processed, the 25% extra time to accompany a scribe can be added to the application.

If a candidate will require 25% extra time in some examinations in which he will not be using a scribe (i.e. a standalone arrangement), separate assessment evidence is needed for each arrangement.

Assessment evidence is not required for a computer reader/reader. The SENCo writes a file note to set out the evidence. It is not possible to add 25% extra time as an option to accompany an application for a computer reader/reader. However, the JCQ asks that the need for 25% extra time alongside a computer reader/reader is always considered. If the candidate requires 25% extra time, then he must meet the published criteria for 25% extra time and the required evidence must be in place to support an on-line application.

9. Is assessment evidence needed for a candidate who requires a reader?

No. For all candidates needing a reader, including those with learning difficulties, the SENCo writes a short concise file note to confirm the nature of the difficulty and that the use of a reader reflects the candidate's normal way of working. An online application for approval must be made using Access Arrangements Online.

10. My student needs a reader and 25% extra time. Can I put the evidence for both arrangements on Form 8?

No, Form 8 is used to detail the evidence for 25% for a candidate with learning difficulties who does not have an EHCP, IDP (in Wales) or SEN Statement (in Northern Ireland). The evidence for a reader is written on a file note.

For a candidate who has an EHCP, IDP or Statement, or a candidate who has communication and interaction needs, sensory and physical needs or social, emotional and mental health needs, the evidence for both 25% extra time and for a reader can be written on the same file note, as long as all of the points are addressed for both arrangements.

11. Can a learner who has English as a second language have a reader on account of his difficulties with the English language?

No. Only those who also have problems in their first language and evidence of learning difficulties and history of need and provision can be considered. See Chapter 18 for further discussion.

12. How do I decide whether a candidate has a reader or a computer reader?

The decision needs to be based on the candidate's normal way of working. A computer reader can be used in exams testing reading and allows the candidate to work independently, which is beneficial. However, it is only acceptable where the candidate is entirely familiar and happy with using reading software and has been using it regularly.

13. How many students can I put in a group to have access to a reader?

This should be determined by the needs of the students. The JCQ says that the group should be no more than 4. You should ensure that the students are not operating at very different levels such that one candidate dominates the reader to the exclusion of access for the others and consider if the students are confident enough to put their hands up and ask for help.

14. How can I decide which scribe arrangement to choose?

A 'scribe' suggests either: a human scribe, use of voice recognition software or use of a word processor with spell-check, grammar-check and/or predictive text enabled. The decision as to which arrangement a candidate uses needs to be based on his current needs and normal way of working. With that in mind, you should opt for the arrangement that gives the candidate the most independence, which still allows him to fully demonstrate his knowledge, and which he is confident using. You should consider them in this order of preference:

1) Word processor (spell-check and grammar-check switched off – i.e. centre-delegated arrangement)
2) Word processor with spell-check, grammar-check, predictive text switched on
3) Voice recognition software
4) Human scribe

15. Can a scribe use a word processor?

Yes. If the scribe is able to type quickly, it can help the candidate to dictate more steadily.

16. What is the centre's position if a candidate demands to use a word processor, or they have a private report stating that a word processor is their normal way of working?

A word processor can be provided where this is the candidate's current way of working and according to the centre's word processor policy, which sets out the criteria for candidates using word processors. You do not have to provide a word processor simply because a student prefers to work that way.

17. Can students bring in their own laptops for use in exams?

No. All word processors must meet JCQ set up guidelines. Equipment must be provided by the centre.

18. Where do I find the list of tests that have been approved for access arrangements assessments?

There is no list of approved tests. The JCQ does not stipulate which tests must be used when assessing for evidence for access arrangements. Some guidance on considerations for assessment tools is provided within Chapter 7 of the JCQ AARA document. However, assessors are expected to use their professional judgement in selecting appropriate tests in line with the assessment criteria for each access arrangement. See Chapter 10 in this Guide for details of some commonly used tests.

19. Do I still need a qualification in assessment if I am using a computer-based test?

Yes. All assessors must hold, as a minimum, a qualification in assessment at (or equivalent to) Level 7 in order to conduct assessments that can provide assessment evidence for access arrangements. Computer-based assessment tools, just like paper-based tests, must be administered by suitably qualified assessors if they are to be used within Form 8 Part 2.

20. Is one below average score enough to provide access arrangements?

No. Assessment evidence by itself does not provide sufficient evidence for access arrangements. There must be centre-based evidence to accompany any test scores, and which is the basis for the testing.

Once the centre-based evidence is in place, some access arrangements require at least one below average score in a specified area as assessment evidence. Other arrangements require a minimum of two scores. For other, higher risk, arrangements, one or more substantially below average scores are needed.

21. What access arrangements are available for students diagnosed with dyscalculia?

The diagnosis itself, as with dyslexia, does not bring any automatic arrangement; and a calculator, which is a common request, is only permitted where it is also available for all candidates to maintain the validity of the qualification. A discrepancy between literacy and maths test results is not sufficient to argue for an arrangement. If cognitive processing difficulties exist, extra time for maths exams might be appropriate. However, any decision needs to take account of the centre-based evidence. You will need to consider carefully whether this is a useful arrangement for the individual and whether the candidate has the strategies in place to help them to use the extra time. Where a maths processing test is used as one of the two measures for 25% extra time, the score must be below average and the extra time can only be used in maths exams.

22. How do colleges obtain a history of provision and evidence of current need?

If a candidate declares a difficulty on application or enrolment, you can request a copy of his existing evidence, or get permission from him to contact his previous school. Under certain conditions, it may be possible to 'roll forward' a Form 8 from another centre, meaning that a new assessment is not required, although centre-based evidence needs to be updated in some circumstances (see Chapter 15).

If the paperwork from the previous centre is not forthcoming, the process needs to start again. It may be possible to telephone the school SENCo and note down any useful data that is provided verbally. The student's reported experience will also be useful, as will the results of any screening tests conducted on entry, early observations of teaching staff using carefully constructed questionnaires and evidence from timed assessments or assignments.

23. A learner has moved into our Sixth Form from Year 11. He had 25% extra time for GCSEs and his AAO approval has not yet expired. Can this be used for his maths GCSE retake in November?

Yes. The learner has remained in the same centre, his exam is at the same level, i.e. GCSE, and the JCQ approval has not yet expired. He is able to have 25% extra time in the November retake without further evidence.

For his GCE exams, the centre-based evidence will need to be updated and his Form 8 will need to be rolled forward. See Chapter 15 for further discussion.

24. Does Form 8 need to be hand-signed?

Form 8 can either be signed by hand or a typed or electronic signature can be used. The same applies to the file note completed by the SENCo and the data protection notice signed by the candidate.

25. Can I use Form 8 Part 1 for all the centre evidence, regardless of whether an assessment is taking place? I would prefer to have all my paperwork in the same format.

No, Form 8 is a profile of learning difficulties. It is only used when an assessment takes place and must be accompanied by Parts 2 and 3.

For candidates who do not need to be assessed, i.e. those who have an EHCP, IDP (in Wales) or SEN Statement (in Northern Ireland) or who have communication and interaction needs, sensory and physical needs or social, emotional and mental health needs, the centre-based evidence is written up by the SENCo as a centre file note. The information that needs to be addressed differs depending on the access arrangements that are required.

Appendix 1: List of Acronyms and Abbreviations

AAO	Access Arrangements Online
AARA	Access Arrangements and Reasonable Adjustments
AB	Awarding Body
ALS	Additional Learning Support
APC	Assessment Practising Certificate
BDA	British Dyslexia Association
BPS	British Psychological Society
CAP	Centre Admin Portal
CPD	Continuing Professional Development
CP	Communication Professional
DfE	Department for Education
DCD	Developmental Coordination Disorder
DSA	Disabled Students Allowance
EAL	English as an Additional Language
EHCP	Education Health and Care Plan
ESP	Education Support Plan
FE	Further Education
FSMQ	Free-Standing Mathematics Qualification
GCSE	General Certificate of Secondary Education
GCE	General Certificate of Education
HADC	Helen Arkell Dyslexia Centre
HCPC	Health and Care Professions Council
HE	Higher Education
IDP	Individual Development Plan
IEP/ILP	Individual Education Plan / Individual Learning Plan
JCQ	Joint Council for Qualifications
LM	Language Modifier
NEA	Non-Examination Assessment
Patoss	Professional Association of Teachers of Students with SpLD
SpLD	Specific Learning Difficulties
SASC	SpLD Assessment Standards Committee
SD	Standard Deviation
SEM	Standard Error of Measurement
SEND CoP	Special Educational Needs and Disability Code of Practice
SS	Standard Score
SEN	Special Educational Needs
SENCo	Special Educational Needs Coordinator
TD	Typically developed
ToD	Teacher of the Deaf

Appendix 2: Accessing Resources to Download

Below is a list of forms and templates introduced in this book which are downloadable from the Patoss website.

Use the following address to access them:
www.patoss-dyslexia.org/AA-6EdResources

Access Arrangements - Information for students and parents template

Converting scaled scores to standard scores

Email template to teachers-support staff

Evidence collection for extra time - online form template

Excel 1 chart to display test scores

Excel 2 Setting up a bar chart to display score results

Extra Time Evidence collection sheet for student

File note template 25% Extra Time or Scribe

File note template Computer reader-reader or Supervised Rest Breaks

File note template Extra Time of over 50%

File note template Extra Time of up to 50%

Form to list students with performance raising concerns

Guidance sheet to complete Form 8

Reference sheet: Evidence requirements for access arrangements

Referral form for teachers-tutors

Roll Forward form 25% Extra Time and/or Scribe

SENCo checklist for AA candidate files

Staff Feedback Access Arrangements

Student's view of Normal Way of Working

Teacher checklist Normal Way of Working

Written work and or exam performance not meeting expectations

Note: These resources are available for the personal use of purchasers of this book.

Additional copies of the book can be purchased from the Patoss website.

Appendix 3: Test References

Academic Achievement Battery (AAB), 2014, Messer, M.A.: PAR, Inc

Access Reading Test 3rd Edition (ART), 2018, McCarthy, C. and Crumpler, M.: RS Assessment from Hodder Education

Adult Reading Test 2nd Edition (ART-2), 2016, Brooks, P., Everatt, J. and Fidler, R.: Pearson Assessment

Beery-Buktenica Developmental Test of Visual-Motor Integration, 6th Edition (Beery VMI), 2010, Beery, K. E., Buktenica, N. A. and Beery, N. A.: Pearson Assessment

British Picture Vocabulary Scale, 3rd Edition (BPVS-3), 2009, Dunn, L. M., Dunn, D. M. and National Foundation for Educational Research: GL Assessment

Comprehensive Test of Phonological Processing, 2nd Edition (CTOPP-2), 2013, Wagner, R. K., Torgesen, J. K., Rashotte, C. A. and Pearson, N. A.: Pro-Ed, Inc

Detailed Assessment of Speed of Handwriting (DASH), 2007, Barnett, A., Henderson, S., Scheib, B. and Schulz, J.: Pearson Education

Detailed Assessment of Speed of Handwriting 17+ (DASH 17+), 2010, Barnett, A., Henderson, S., Scheib, B. and Schulz, J.: Pearson Education

Developmental Test of Visual Perception-Adolescent and Adult: Second Edition (DTVP-A:2), 2021, Reynolds, C., Pearson, N., and Voress, J.: Pro-Ed, Inc

Diagnostic Reading Analysis, 3rd Edition (DRA 3), 2019, Crumpler, M. and McCarthy, C.: Hodder Education

Diagnostic Spelling Tests, 2006, Crumpler, M. and McCarthy, C.: Hodder Education

Dyslexia Portfolio, 2008, Turner, M.: GL Assessment

Exact, 2009, Ferrier, J. and Horne, J.: GL Assessment

Expressive Vocabulary Test, 3rd Edition (EVT-2), 2019, Williams, K.: Pearson Assessment

Feifer Assessment of Mathematics (FAM), 2015, Feifer, S. G.: PAR, Inc

Feifer Assessment of Reading (FAR), 2015, Feifer, S. G. and Gerhardstein Nader, R.: PAR, Inc

Full Range Test of Visual Motor Integration (FRTVMI), 2005, Hammill, D., Pearson, N, Voress, J. and Reynolds, C.: Pro-Ed, Inc

Gray Oral Reading Tests, 5th Edition (GORT-5), 2012, Wiederholt, J. L. and Bryant, B. R.: Pro-ed, Inc

Gray Silent Reading Test (GSRT), 2000, Wiederholt, J. L. and Bryant, R.: Pro-Ed, Inc

Helen Arkell Spelling Test, 2nd Edition (HAST-2), 2012, Caplan, M., Bark, C. and McLean, B.: Helen Arkell Dyslexia Centre

Hodder Group Reading Tests (HGRT) II, 2007, Vincent, D. and Crumpler, M.: Hodder Education

Kaufman Test of Educational Achievement, 3rd Edition (KTEA-3), 2014, Kaufman, A.S. and Kaufman, N.L.: Pearson Assessment

New Group Reading Test (NGRT), 3rd Edition, 2010, Burge, B., Styles, B., Brsyska, B., Cooper, L., Shamsan, Y., Saltini, F. and Twist, L.: GL Assessment

Peabody Picture Vocabulary Test, 5th Edition (PPVT-5), 2018, Dunn, L.M. and Dunn, D.M.: Pearson Assessment

Rapid Automatized Naming and Rapid Alternating Stimulus Tests (RAN/RAS), 2005, Wolf, M. and Bridge Denckla, M.: Pro-Ed, Inc

Ravens Progressive Matrices & Vocabulary Scales, 2008, Raven, J. C., Court, J. H. and Raven, J.: Pearson Assessment

Lucid Recall (Second Edition), 2015, St. Clair-Thompson, H.: GL Assessment

Single Word Spelling Test (SWST), 2001, Sacre, L. and Masterton, J.: GL Assessment

SPaRCS Test, 2017, James, K., Good, R. and James, T.: Education Elephant

Suffolk Reading Scale Digital (SRS Digital), 2008, Hagley, F.: GL Assessment

Symbol Digit Modalities Test (SDMT), 1973, Smith, A.: Western Psychological Services

TAPS-4 – A Language Processing Skills Assessment, 2018, Martin, N., Brownell, R. and Hamaguchi, P.: Academic Therapy Publications

Test of Information Processing Skills (TIPS), 2009, Webster, R.: Academic Therapy Publications

Test of Memory and Learning, 2nd Edition (TOMAL-2), 2007, Reynolds, C. R. and Voress, J. K.: Pro-ed, Inc

Test of Silent Word Reading Fluency, 2nd Edition (TOSWRF-2), 2014, Mather, N., Hammill, D., Allen, E. and Roberts, R.:Pro-Ed, Inc

Test of Visual Motor Skills, 3rd Edition (TVMS-3), 2010, Martin, N.: Academic Therapy Publications

Test of Word Reading Efficiency, 2nd Edition (TOWRE-2), 2012, Torgesen, J., Wagner, R. and Rashotte, C.: Pro-ed, Inc

Vernon Graded Word Spelling Test, 3rd Edition, 2006, Vernon, P. E., Revised by Crumpler, M. and McCarthy, C.: Hodder Education

Vocabulary Assessment Scales – Expressive and Receptive (VAS-E, VAR-R), 2013, Nader, R.G.: Par, Inc

Wechsler Individual Achievement Test, 3rd UK Edition (WIAT-III-UK), 2017, Wechsler, D.: Pearson Assessment

Wechsler Individual Achievement Test, 3rd UK Edition for Teachers (WIAT-III-UK-T), 2018, Wechsler, D.: Pearson Assessment

Wide Range Achievement Test 5th Edition (WRAT-5), 2017, Robertson, G. J.: Psychological Assessment Resources, Inc.

Wide Range Achievement Test - Expanded (WRAT-E), 2001, Wilkinson, G. S. and Robertson, G. J.: Psychological Assessment Resources, Inc.

Wide Range Assessment of Memory and Learning, 2nd Edition (WRAML-2), 2003, Sheslow, D. and Adams, W.: Psychological Assessment Resources, Inc

Wide Range Intelligence Test (WRIT), 2000, Glutting, J., Adams, W. and Sheslow, D.: Psychological Assessment Resources, Inc.

Woodcock Reading Mastery Tests, 3rd Edition (WRMT-III), 2011, Woodcock, R. W.: Pearson Assessment

Woodcock-Johnson IV Tests of Achievement (WJ IV ACH) UK and Ireland edition, 2018, Schrank F.A., Mather N. and McGrew K.S.: Riverside Insights

Woodcock-Johnson IV Tests of Cognitive Abilities (WJ IV COG), 2014, Schrank F.A., Mather N. and McGrew K.S.: Riverside Insights

York Assessment of Reading for Comprehension Secondary (YARC), 2010, Snowling, M. J., Stothard, S. E., Clance, P., Bowyer-Crane, C. D., Harrington, A., Truelove, E. and Hulme, C.: GL Assessment

Appendix 4: Patoss AAA: Assessing for Access Arrangements Qualification

The Patoss AAA postgraduate course provides training in assessment for access arrangements.

The Patoss AAA course meets the **JCQ requirements** for access arrangements assessor training and is equivalent to Level 7. Successful completion of the course will enable participants to carry out assessments for access arrangements and complete JCQ Form 8 Part 2.

The course involves 200 hours of study, consisting of live, online sessions, recorded presentations delivered through the online platform, formative and extension tasks, and independent study. Throughout the course each delegate has a designated course tutor who advises on and marks formative tasks and assessments.

The course is delivered in two units, each a term in length and comprising four live online sessions:

- **Unit 1, Professional Practice Underpinnings**, examines the underlying causes of the challenges experienced by learners with cognition and learning needs.
- **Unit 2, Professional Practice**, explores basic psychometrics, commonly used assessment tools, and the principles underlying the assessment and application process, equipping delegates with the skills and knowledge required to undertake the role of exam access arrangements assessor.

Assessment is through a combination of written and practical tasks.

Entry requirements:
- Minimum undergraduate degree and teaching qualification (e.g. QTS) **and/or** Level 5 specialist teaching qualification in SpLD / Dyslexia
- Delegates are also required to have access to students (Y9 –Y13 or FE) for the observed assessment and access to assessment materials.

The course is delivered twice each year, beginning in September and January. It can also be provided as an On-Site Training Event.

Holders of the Patoss AAA and a specialist teaching qualification will be eligible to enrol onto our PPAR postgraduate course leading to an SpLD Assessment Practising Certificate.

Contact Patoss for further information: info@patoss-dyslexia.org